A RIVER RAT'S GUIDE TO THE THOUSAND ISLANDS

D1596825

A RIVER RAT'S GUIDE TO THE THOUSAND ISLANDS

SHAWN THOMPSON

The BOSTON
MILLS PRESS

CANADIAN CATALOGUING IN PUBLICATION DATA

Thompson, Shawn, 1951–
A river rat's guide to the Thousand Islands

Includes bibliographical references and index.
ISBN 1-55046-173-7

1. Thousand Islands (N.Y. and Ont.) - Tours.
2. Thousand Islands (N.Y. and Ont.) - Guidebooks. I. Title.

FC3095.T43A3 1996   917.13'7044   C96-930340-8
F1059.T43T46 1996

First published in 1996 by
The Boston Mills Press
132 Main Street
Erin, Ontario, Canada
N0B 1T0
Tel 519 833-2407
Fax 519 833-2195

An affiliate of
Stoddart Publishing Company Ltd.
34 Lesmill Road
North York, Ontario, Canada
M3B 2T6

All photographs by the author,
except p. 22 (Jack Chiang) and p. 29 (*The Kingston Whig-Standard*)

Design by Mary Firth
Printed in Canada

The publisher gratefully acknowledges the support of the Canada Council and Ontario Arts Council in
the development of writing and publishing in Canada.

Page 2 photo: *A great blue heron about to eat a fish.*

CONTENTS

To my son, Pearce

INTRODUCTION

I T WASN'T ALWAYS the way it is now in the Thousand Islands.

Take a period of time such as the War of 1812, when Britain was at war with the United States. Charles Darwin was just a babe then, as were Abe Lincoln and Charles Dickens. The steam engine was a recent innovation and ships were pushed by the power of the wind in their sails. Canada was still a colony of Great Britain — small, vulnerable, unsure of itself. In 1813, an American fleet gathered at an island near what today is the small American town of Cape Vincent, not far from Kingston. It was preparing to invade Canada. Of course, the British already knew about the Americans. Their plans were no secret to the British. The islanders — nobody could control them then and nobody has been able to since — had warned the British. And so the British sent one of their biggest troublemakers, Lieutenant-Colonel Red George Macdonell, down the river to intercept the invasion. A gale arose on the St. Lawrence. Macdonell, daring that power, took his boats through the storm. They went down the rapids without a guide to meet the American flotilla — which was slow to materialize because the American boats had taken such a beating on the river. The river was acknowledged as an old and palpable force then. The times are different, but the river has changed little. It's still an incredible force in people's lives.

As long as I've lived in Gananoque — which, incidentally, lost its bridge during an American raid in the War of 1812 — I've learned how it

The river freezes in the wintertime to form a bridge of ice that's easy to cross.

feels to live beside a river as old as the St. Lawrence. I came from a city, landlocked except for a dirty little rag of a river. Coming from that city to the Thousand Islands, it felt as though I had arrived from a foreign country. The city was too large to feel familiar, like a neighbourhood. But the people of the river knew where they were. They had the privilege of being in a particular place for years and years. The river was theirs and they were at home.

From Wolfe Island in the west to Three Sisters Island in the east, the Thousand Islands behaves like a little nation unto itself. This place has evolved from the parts of itself that it was able to protect from the influence of other things. On the river, that influence has been the politicians and the bureaucrats of two countries. They tried to make the islands fit their rules and failed miserably. For that, you and I should be grateful. Something has been left untouched for us. The area has resisted being simply a copy of other places for hundreds of years. The people here can still think for themselves. They're not duplicates of something else.

Before the Europeans and the Loyalists came, many of them from places that no longer felt like home, the Thousand Islands had been a frontier that shifted from one group of Indians to another. The Indians, with a few exceptions, never stayed the whole year. When the French arrived in the late 1600s, the best they could do was to build a few forts along the St. Lawrence River. Distance was measured by the sound of a cannon being fired. A flash of gunpowder and life made sense.

During the War of 1812, the upper end of the river wasn't tame enough to be the scene of one decent battle. Since the 1800s, smugglers have thrived here better than bureaucrats. And for a long time — before there were bridges — the distinctions between the two sides of the river were blurred by migrations and marriages and one simple fact: nobody cared where the imaginary line was between Canada and the United States.

In the 1800s, the great influx of the Europeans started. Trees were chopped down, rock was dug out of quarries, corn was planted. On the south side of the river, a republic formed, with river people along its border; on the north side, a country emerged that would one day be a democracy, unrepublican in nature, with more river people along its border. And, in spite of the border between the two sides, the people were united. They came together on the river. It may have been a collection of rocks and islands, with no flag or currency or constitution, but it acted like a country.

The local citizens, the Thousand Islanders, know that this country has a law of its own, particularly whenever a bureaucracy or a government tries to impose its rules on them. We say that nobody tells the fish when they've crossed the border, that nobody divides the ducks between theirs and ours. We think it's all just one big river. We think our country simply exists, without bothering to explain the logic of that belief or analyzing why people here don't think the same way that they do in cities. The river, as we say, becomes a part of us. You can smell it when you get close to it on a hot day — the seaweedy smell of something rank and old and fecund. You can taste the wind too, somewhat brassy on a quick, bright afternoon. You watch the water fill with light as the sun comes up; you see it drain of that brilliance as the sun goes down. And you feel like it's happening to you.

The rest of this book will give you a taste of my adopted country, the grand old duchy of the Thousand Islands, an archipelago of green seas and hidden shoals and a few trappers in slow, battered boats.

BY RIVER OR BY RAIL

The common way to approach the river is by car, travelling around the edge, in a circumspect way, by road. That's quite a difference from the days when most travel was by boat. And so, in order to appreciate the changes that the communities along the river — and, ultimately, the river itself — have gone through, you have to understand the transition from boats to railways to paved roads.

In the late 1700s, Kingston, now the largest city in the area, was founded at the junction of Lake Ontario and the St. Lawrence River. That was where, by the logic of rivers and seas at the time, the military and economic power lay. The rapids on the St. Lawrence River bottled up ships in the Great Lakes and the upper section of the river. That created the need for a shipbuilding industry and for a port, such as Kingston, where cargo could be loaded and unloaded. The islands near Kingston, such as Garden Island, and communities on the American side of the river, such as Clayton, also started building ships. By the 1830s Kingston and the islands were set on a course that would have made them a major centre on the continent. Kingston was only a few years away from being chosen as the capital of the colony of Canada. Business on the river was thriving and the two sides of the river were bound together by trade. And so, in this period, when influence was derived from great rivers, the future greatness of Kingston and the islands seemed assured.

But then there came a series of changes that affected the St. Lawrence and undermined the economy based on the river. The two most important changes were the growth of the railways and the construction of the canals of the mid-1800s. These killed many of the economic advantages of the upper St. Lawrence, although the shipbuilding industry held on through the decline during the late 1800s. Kingston, prophetically, helped to signal its end as a port city when its factories started to produce the steam locomotives of the new technology. The largest industry of the city in the late 1800s was the locomotive plant. Then, during the Depression, the bridge was built across the river at Ivy Lea, further weakening the influence of ferries and boat transportation. The final blow came in 1959 with the opening of the St. Lawrence Seaway. The seaway made Kingston obsolete as a port city because large freighters could pass between the ocean and the Great Lakes unimpeded.

The islands followed the same downward path as the port towns and the shipbuilding industry. Before the railroads and bridges, the farmers on

the islands had advantages that farmers inland didn't have. The island farmers could sell their goods locally by boat or send them to a city by
steamboat. They didn't have to struggle with primitive roads, since they
could travel with ease on the river. In the wintertime, when others were
impeded by snow, the river froze and opened up the countryside even
more. People travelled across the ice on skates, by horse and wagon, and
even on foot. The governor-general arrived in the new capital town of
Kingston by sleigh from the American side. The most ingenious use of ice
on the river was in Montreal where, for three years in the 1880s, tracks were
laid across the frozen river for trains. But however ingenious the connections to the islands, the railroads and the bridges and the new paved roads
were the end of them.

In the process of all this, Kingston turned its back on the river. In the
last few years it has reclaimed some of its waterfront and made it attractive,
but it has also lost its culture as a port city. Its people, who came here by
boat and once inhaled the fresh winds of the open water, became institu-
tionalized, either in government departments, universities and colleges, or
prisons. They became city people rather than river people. Today Kingston,
for all its accomplishments, lives in a world separate from the islands lying
outside it.

FINALLY, SOME DIRECTIONS

It would be a shame for you to come to the Thousand Islands and not have
to wrestle with the river. The St. Lawrence shouldn't be ignored, however
remote rivers have become from the way we live and think today. For that
reason, I've written a book that will take you down backroads and get you
closer to the water. I've included just enough brick walls to do justice to
the towns on the St. Lawrence, but the real fun is in riding the ferries and
crossing the bridges and looking at the river from different angles.

At this point, if your time is limited to a day or two, you'll have to
make some choices. You can take the car ferry to Wolfe Island and scout the

countryside there, or cross the big bridges that tether the two sides of the river together at Ivy Lea, or enjoy the river from the coastal roads, of which the best view is along the Thousand Islands Parkway between Gananoque and Brockville. Island roads in general aren't a good way to see the river. They were often built through the centre of an island to connect the farms on the shoreline in simple, straight lines. They weren't made for sightseers who'd like to follow the edge of the river. The islands of Wolfe and Simcoe, for instance, have mainly interior roads and all you'll see there is flat farm fields.

Communities such as Brockville, Ogdensburg, and Alexandria Bay have good vantage points where you can park your car, get out, and watch the freighters pass. If you have kids, these are also good places to let them run wild for a while, with playgrounds near the water. The small towns and lodges also have lists of fishing guides who can get you out onto the river into obscure spots that you'd never see otherwise. Even if you aren't interested in fishing, these men are fun to talk to and know what's happening on the river.

Stopping at one of the public beaches is another way of exploring the area. The beach at Mallorytown Landing has a historic wreck in a pavilion and some of the action on the river can be glimpsed from there. Many of the American beaches are also good places for contemplating the river. And don't forget this: a beach — which is one of the few places left where you can still read a book in peace — may help to remind you of a wonderful old truth: for centuries people have been baptized in rivers like this one to mark a transformation in their lives.

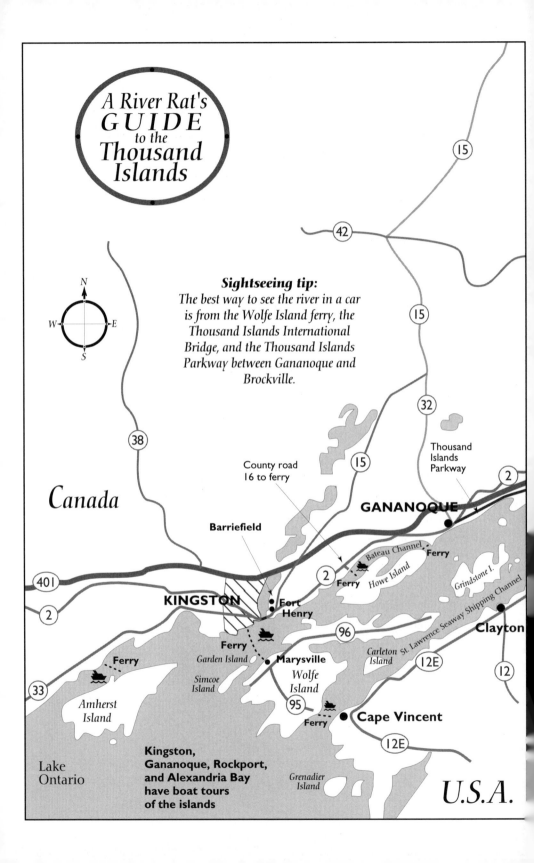

A River Rat's GUIDE to the Thousand Islands

Sightseeing tip:
The best way to see the river in a car is from the Wolfe Island ferry, the Thousand Islands International Bridge, and the Thousand Islands Parkway between Gananoque and Brockville.

Canada

County road 16 to ferry

Barriefield

Thousand Islands Parkway

GANANOQUE

Bateau Channel **Ferry**

Ferry   Howe Island

Grindstone I.

St. Lawrence Seaway Shipping Channel

Clayton

KINGSTON   Fort Henry

Ferry

Garden Island   **Marysville**

Simcoe Island

Ferry

Amherst Island

Wolfe Island

Carleton Island

Cape Vincent

Grenadier Island

Lake Ontario

Kingston, Gananoque, Rockport, and Alexandria Bay have boat tours of the islands

U.S.A.

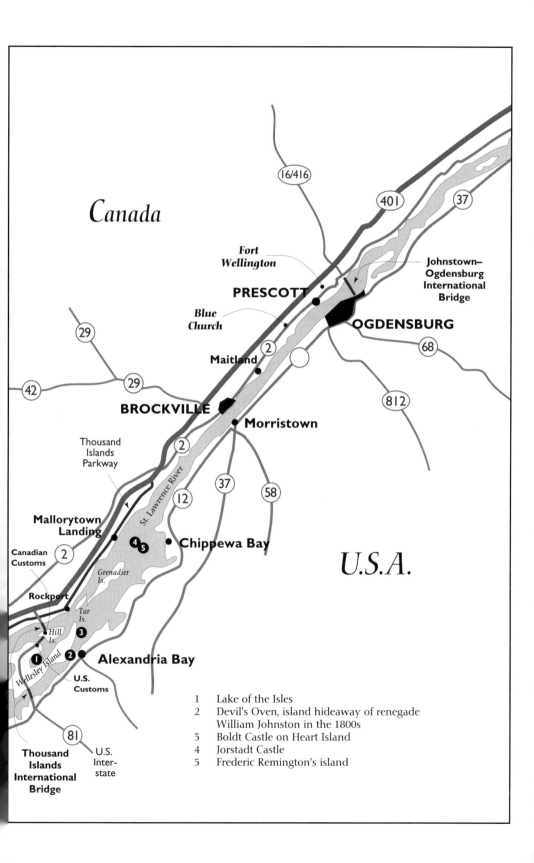

Canada

U.S.A.

16/416
401
37

Fort Wellington

PRESCOTT

Johnstown–
Ogdensburg
International
Bridge

Blue
Church

OGDENSBURG

29

68

Maitland

2

29

42

812

BROCKVILLE

Morristown

Thousand
Islands
Parkway

2

St. Lawrence River

37

58

12

Mallorytown
Landing

Grenadier
Is.

Chippewa Bay

❹❺

Canadian
Customs

2

Rockport

Tar
Is.

❸

Hill
Is.

❶

❷●

Wellesley Island

Alexandria Bay

U.S.
Customs

1   Lake of the Isles
2   Devil's Oven, island hideaway of renegade
    William Johnston in the 1800s
3   Boldt Castle on Heart Island
4   Jorstadt Castle
5   Frederic Remington's island

81

U.S.
Inter-
state

Thousand
Islands
International
Bridge

*P*ainting a ship in the dry dock at Kingston.

KINGSTON

GREAT EXPECTATIONS

I N 1842, CHARLES DICKENS arrived by steamboat in the new capital of
Canada. The capital was Kingston and it was a remarkable place to be at the
time. The parliament had been inaugurated in town the year before. The
port was busy with ships. The town was full of soldiers and immigrants and
politicians. Dickens, a product of the city himself, preferred a civilized spot
like this to the ragged wilderness lying outside.[1] To add to the excitement,
a sea monster had been spotted off Gull Point. Kingston had everything.

Dickens was a typical Victorian tourist. One of the attractions of the
town for him was the dock area, awash with sailors and taverns. Dickens
also wanted to see the most important buildings. Those were the fort on the
other side of the Cataraqui River and the penitentiary. In old Kingston, a
great deal of ingenuity went into designing and building forts, and prisons,
and lunatic asylums. Victorians appreciated a good penitentiary.

Dickens was enchanted by the prison, and by a prisoner he found
there. In the travelogue he wrote afterwards he spent more time describing
the "admirable jail" than the town. And most of his attention in the prison
was taken by a prisoner named Eunice Whiting. She was a small, twenty-
year-old woman with dark grey eyes and auburn hair. Officially, she had
been convicted of stealing a horse when she was seventeen. But the truth
was that she'd helped in the 1837 Rebellion. It's possible that Dickens felt

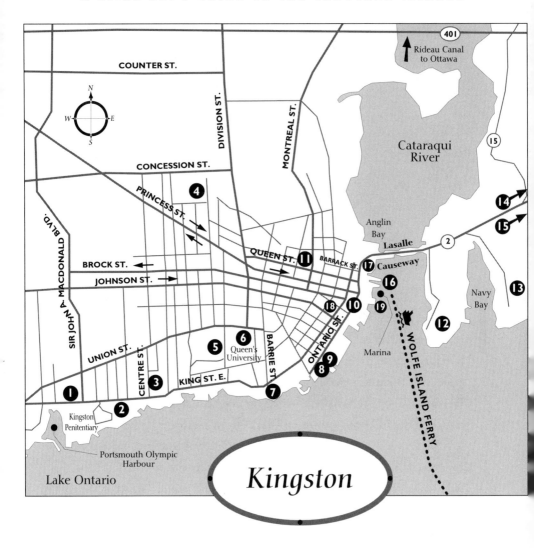

1   Correctional Service of Canada Museum
2   Kingston Archaeological Centre
3   Bellevue House National Historic Park
4   International Ice Hockey Federation Museum
5   Agnes Etherington Art Centre (Queen's University)
6   Miller Museum of Geology and Mineralogy (Queen's University)
7   Murney Tower Museum
8   Pump House Steam Museum
9   Marine Museum of the Great Lakes
10 City Hall / Farmers' Market
11 Princess of Wales Own Regiment Museum
12 RMC Museum and the site of Fort Frederick
13 Fort Henry
14 Canadian Forces Communications and Electronics Museum
15 MacLachlan Woodworking Museum
16 Wolfe Island ferry dock at the end of Barrack Street
17 Tete–du–Pont Barracks and site of Fort Frontenac
18 St. George's Cathedral
19 Boat tours

a romantic twinge for her. She was a spirited woman who followed her heart. Dickens wrote that she had "a lovely face" with "a devil lurking in her bright eye." He described how she dressed as a boy and stole horses to carry messages for the insurgents.

After four days in Kingston, Dickens left by steamboat. The one he picked sounded like a person, since it was named the *Henry Gildersleeve*, after a Kingston shipbuilder. The *Henry Gildersleeve* stopped in places such as Gananoque and Brockville and Prescott as it went along the St. Lawrence. The steamboats of the day brought luxury and grace to the river. Victorians such as Dickens liked to praise a boat for its stained-glass windows and rich divans, as though it were a cathedral or a fine hotel. As a reward for the elegance of his boat, the captain might be given a silver snuff box. After a voyage on a steamboat, Victorian travellers turned their impressions into books and travelogues that romanticized the new country. That, in turn, influenced the flood of immigration.

The *Henry Gildersleeve*, on which Dickens sailed, had the typical life of a steamboat. It had its glory days with wealthy tourists, then it was delegated to more humble jobs, such as hauling masses of poor Irish immigrants up the river to places like Kingston. And then, with the rise of the railways, it was given the real dirty work. It was converted, a decade after Dickens's visit, into an ordinary tugboat. The *Henry Gildersleeve* also had the typical bad luck of its breed: its shafts were forever breaking, and the boiler blew up, scalding two people.

After leaving Kingston, Dickens travelled through the Thousand Islands. He praised the islands for their variety and number and different sizes. Some were as small as "dimples," he said. Then he came to the rapids, which were a tourist attraction at the time. The rapids would ultimately be tamed by the construction of the St. Lawrence Seaway. But Dickens could still write in his travelogue about the excitement of the rough water. He said, "In the afternoon we shot down some rapids where the river boiled and bubbled strangely, and where the force and headlong violence of the current were tremendous." By comparison, Dickens hadn't enjoyed his trip on the Mississippi. The St. Lawrence was "a noble stream," he wrote, but the Mississippi was "beastliest river in the world."

As for the port of Kingston that Dickens left behind, its fortunes were changing. It would lose the stature it had when the writer visited it. The navy yard in Kingston had already closed a few years earlier, and during the next few decades the military influence on Kingston and the Thousand Islands would dwindle. Shortly after Dickens's visit, Kingston lost its status as the capital of the country. The town was a capital city for less than three years. It was dangerous to have the capital of a country near the border where it could be attacked by Americans. Dickens made the observation common at the time that "the town is much too close upon the frontier to be held long." The British were well aware of the risk, as were the Americans. During the 1837 Rebellion, the Americans had planned to cross the ice from the United States and take the settlement. And so, for a number of reasons, Kingston became a town again. It lost its importance, but not its charm.

DOWNTOWN TOUR

The quickest way to get a measure of the old grandeur of Kingston is to start a walking tour from the city hall. In the river across from the city hall is a stone defense tower from the 1840s. From here, go south on Ontario Street past the Prince George Hotel (circa 1809, rebuilt 1849), the haunt of the most flamboyant rumrunners and bootleggers during Prohibition days. Then turn west on Clarence Street to the soberest of structures, the Customs House (1856-58), and south on King Street in the direction of the dome of St. George's Cathedral. The buildings take you back in time to the beginning of Canada as a nation and give you a sense of the enormous ambitions of the people who originally lived in Kingston.

These few streets — and the ones that radiate from them, taking you deeper into the city — also give you a chance to see how much of

Kingston was built of limestone. From the beginning, limestone gave the place its air of distinction, and its ghostly blue hue. It was out of this rock, in the form of the town hall, the churches, and the penitentiary, that the people gave shape to their aspirations. And it was this same rock that preserved the old part of the city against change. What is built of rock stays put.

CITY HALL
(1843–1844)

This building is impressive, no doubt about it. And it's even more impressive when you think about the audacity of erecting it in the mid-1800s in the middle of a wilderness. It was topped off with a big dome that would eventually be echoed in other buildings across the skyline of Kingston. Part of this particular dome was supposed to be — although it never was — an observatory for gazing upwards, from streets that were darker in those days, toward the light of the stars.

The structure — which you can enter and explore, staircase by staircase — was built, like the fort across the Cataraqui River, for a harbour community, with its back forever turned to the town growing behind it. The lighted circle of the clock on the dome served for years as a beacon to ships.

Inside, the interior reflects the maritime influence on the city through the craftsmanship of the shipbuilders.[2] There's also a stained-glass window dedicated to a sixteen-year-old sailor who died during the great naval battle of Jutland in 1916. The sailor, a gunner, remained at his post while those around him were dying. Maybe nobody cares about the battle of Jutland anymore, but the idea of duty and courage should still be worth something.

When the structure was built it was said to be the finest building in Canada. Fortifications and a battery were once in front of it, and the magnificence of the building has led to a debate over the years about what the builders had in mind. Was the building an attempt to lure the parliament of the country here permanently? Or were the builders merely drunk with a sense of the inflated importance of the place? In any event, by the time the building was completed in 1844, the parliament had decided to move to Montreal. The city hall created an enormous debt for the community because its construction was premised on the tax revenue from a capital city. When Kingston lost its bid to have the parliament remain here, property values fell, tax revenue dropped, and the debt climbed. In the end, the city hall has a grandeur unusual for a town the size that old Kingston was.

ST. GEORGE'S ANGLICAN CATHEDRAL

(1825, REBUILT 1899–1901)

There are plenty of wonderful church buildings in Kingston, some of them more elaborate and graceful outside than this one. It looks, with its big dome and pillars, rather sober and austere, like a compressed version of the city hall. However, for all its austerity, the structure played a glamorous role in the country. In 1792, eight years after the Loyalists started settling here, the original St. George's cathedral was opened. The same year the creation of Upper Canada was proclaimed in the church. The original building had to be replaced, in 1825, by a new St. George's. Then, in 1899, a fire destroyed everything but the limestone walls, which were used to rebuild the church.

The cathedral began under the leadership of the first Anglican clergyman in Upper Canada, the Reverend John Stuart. In those days, the church and the military worked together. The pastor was a missionary to the Mohawks in the Thirteen Colonies and chaplain for the King's Royal Regiment of New York. When the American Revolution broke out, he urged his Mohawk congregation to join the King's side. He was detained and treated as a prisoner, then exchanged for an American officer held prisoner. By this time, Stuart wanted to come to the new settlement in the wilderness at the Cataraqui River. That would allow him to continue his work among the Mohawk allies who were moving to the area. It was here, with help from the Mohawk leader Joseph Brant, that he translated the

Gospel of Mark into the Mohawk language. That gospel begins with a voice crying in the wilderness to prepare the way of the Lord. And then it says, recalling the importance of rivers, "They were baptized by him in the river Jordan."

In front of the altar of St. George's is the burial vault of Lord Sydenham. He was appointed the first governor-general of Canada after it was united, in 1841, into what was called at the time a province. Sydenham annoyed some local people because he enjoyed earthly pleasures so much. He was originally driven from the church by a dull sermon, swearing he'd never return. After his death, he was brought back against his will and put in the vault. Sydenham was the man who made Kingston the capital of Canada. It was intended that his role be commemorated with a statue of the man on top of the dome of the city hall. However, that, like many things in life, never materialized.

THE WATERFRONT

The old waterfront and port of Kingston have mostly disappeared over the years under the layers of change, like the ancient civilization of Atlantis sinking below the waves. Up until the Second World War, the waterfront was a noisy, dirty, industrial zone, which drew people fascinated by the technology of the time. Large lake freighters docked at the waterfront, where large numbers of train engines and steel ships were built. Old men remember sneaking down here at night as boys. They were ushered inside the great hull of a freighter by the cook and given dinner and a tour. When the ships left Kingston, particularly the ones carrying grain, they picked up the humblest residents of this city and of any city — rats. Some of the descendants of these rats still linger under the streets in the ancient sewer pipes. Occasionally they swagger into homes or burrow up through lawns. It seems that a city isn't a city without rats.

There are some good vantage points along the waterfront, particularly in front of the city hall and further along, by Queen's University. It's rare that

The Kingston city hall on the waterfront.

this stretch of water isn't windy, since Kingston has an unusual thermal effect. On a blustery day, the water gets as rough as the old rapids downriver. Where there's wind, of course, there are sailboats and windsurfers to watch.

MARINE MUSEUM OF THE GREAT LAKES

This is almost sacred ground for ship lovers. Wooden ships were built here in the late 1700s, and between 1888 and 1892, a dry dock was established, with Sir John A. Macdonald laying the cornerstone. Then, in 1910, a modern shipyard was opened.

Working on the steel ships was a tough job in those days. The men worked long hours outside, through the heat and the cold. The workers heated the rivets in little pots of fire. Then they tossed the red-hot rivets to the men who hammered them into place to hold the steel plates. Sometimes it was so cold in the wintertime that a worker would heat a steel plate in the fire and stand on it to keep his feet warm. Refitting the old metal ships had other distractions, such as rats that grew to the size of small cats. The workers just kicked the rats aside and kept on working. Men also died at the shipyard, from time to time, in accidents, crushed and mangled by the steel machinery. There's a story about a small boy waiting at the gate for the father who would never return.

A total of one hundred and eight metal ships were either built or refitted here. To get a sense of the size of the operation, consider that, during the First World War, over a thousand men worked in the shipyard constructing trawlers and minesweepers. During the Second World War, even more men, over 1,500, worked on twelve corvettes and a minesweeper. The museum on the old shipbuilding site focuses on the Great Lakes and shipping, with new exhibitions every year.

ONE BIG WARSHIP

One of the factors of the War of 1812 was a monstrous 112-gun warship built by the British in Kingston. At that time, Kingston was the home of the British fleet and the purpose of the fortifications was to defend the navy yard. Since the British built their warships at Kingston, the Commodore of the Great Lakes, a navy officer from the Napoleonic Wars called Sir James Lucas Yeo, built the great warship the *St. Lawrence* here. That prompted the Americans to try and build an even bigger, more powerful ship.

At this time the big British ship caught the attention of one of the biggest irritants the British had during the war. His name was William Johnston. He had been a merchant in Kingston until he was thrown into prison. He was in trouble for either acting as a spy or for insubordination to the military authorities. Whatever it was, he didn't like the way that other people wanted to regulate his life. As a renegade, he became part of the folklore of the islands. Johnston was glorified by some as a buccaneer, reviled by others as a thief and marauder. He raided ships and farmhouses and was able to elude the authorities by hiding in the islands. He must have been a man of great imagination. He thought that he could sink the *St. Lawrence* with a homemade torpedo. That didn't work, because the ship sailed before he could find it. Later, he burned a ship called the *Sir Robert Peel*, in a bungled attempt to steal it.

After the war, the *St. Lawrence*, never having fired any of its guns in battle, stayed in Kingston. The ship was a prisoner of the river, since the rapids downriver prevented it from escaping to the sea. In the wintertime, when the ship was locked in the ice, it was used as a barracks for the officers and men. Then, in the 1830s, the great ship was sold to a merchant in Kingston for twenty-five pounds, the price of a good cow. The merchant used it for a floating coal shed, until it broke loose in a storm and sank, joining other British and French naval ships of the period. The ship sank near the shore and can be seen through the water on a calm day. Commodore Yeo didn't fare much better than his ship; he died in Africa at thirty-five years of age.

By the mid-1800s the navies of the Great Lakes were gone. Great Britain and the United States had agreed at the end of the War of 1812 to prohibit navies inside the continent. The ships were left to rot, and during the cholera epidemic of 1832 were blamed for contaminating the air and for causing fever, ague and malaria. This, of course, happened at a time when one popular cure for cholera was to bleed people.

TETE–DU–PONT BARRACKS
(CIRCA 1820–1830)

All that you can see of this structure is mainly the outside wall, which may or may not be very satisfying, but this is a place of history. The French built Fort Frontenac near here in 1673, under Louis de Buade, Comte de Frontenac and de Palluau. The fort was also a trading centre and mission to the Indians. The location, at Cataraqui, had crucial importance for the

French, as it would later for the British, in attempting to control the interior of the continent.

The French era at Cataraqui ended in 1758 when the British gathered as many small boats as they could muster and sailed here to attack Fort Frontenac. It was a good time for the British and a bad time for the French. In less than a year, General Wolfe would defeat the French and end their proprietorship of Canada. At Cataraqui, the British used their cannons to smash the walls of the French fort. The walls were built of the same limestone that would become in a few years a British fort and a British town.

When the British moved their naval base from Carleton Island, at the U.S. border, to Kingston, they built a fortified barracks here on the west side of the river. In an attack, the barracks with its own battery would have been part of the defences. The original officers' barracks is still here and the old British officers' mess is still used for its original purpose. Part of the wall belongs to the original fortification. The complex is used by the Canadian Armed Forces for military instruction.

LA SALLE CAUSEWAY
(1916–1917)

The causeway has been a part of the landscape for so long that it's hard to think of a time without it. And yet, in 1829, the first wooden bridge was opened from Kingston across the Cataraqui River. The work included a drawbridge strong enough to support artillery carriages and had planks that could be removed for defence. The wooden bridge was constructed, as a nervous traveller said, "on loose stone piers...[over] troubled and deep water." The La Salle Causeway, which came a century later and wasn't built as loosely, got its name from René-Robert Cavelier de La Salle, the first commandant of the French fort at Cataraqui. La Salle was the adventuresome soul who explored the Mississippi River. He saw the French fort finished here and was granted a seigneury by King Louis XIV in exchange for maintaining the military post. In the process of constructing the La Salle Causeway, the builders created one of the nicest ways of looking at the city and the open water. The view is a reward for the people who drive this road every day. They start their day and end it by looking to see what the river is doing.

FORT HENRY

(1832–1836)

The sheer size of this fort, sitting on a lofty hill, is worth experiencing. The hill, with its steep slope, has been used by tobogganers for over one hundred and fifty years. Once you get inside the fort, the heavy walls may seem a bit overpowering, like being locked inside a prison. That's understandable, since years ago people were locked up here. More people have tried — and succeeded — in breaking out of the fort than have attempted to storm it and break in.

In the late 1700s, the British set up a naval base and fortifications here. The fort began later, as a hasty log structure in 1813, at the outbreak of war with the United States. It was an unpleasant time to be in the wilderness of Cataraqui and a fort would have felt particularly safe. Among the other problems, there were swamps that people said were ruining their health, and a British officer complained in 1813 that they were "on the point of being eaten alive by the hungry wood rats as soon as they shall have disposed of our provisions."

The fort was built too late to be used during the War of 1812, but once the stone walls went up in the 1830s, it was handy as a prison during the Rebellion of 1837. Prisoners from the Battle of the Windmill at Prescott were brought to Kingston, where eleven were hanged. Hanging wasn't an unusual punishment of the time, since a man still went to the gallows for stealing a horse. Compassion for the men sentenced to be hanged dwindled after a list was found among the invaders of the important people *they* wanted to hang in Prescott. It seemed that these invaders

*F*ort Henry, Kingston.

had murder on their minds. But when the prisoners were to be hanged, sympathy flared again. After the eleven rebels were hanged, the citizens of the Midland district complained about the cost of building a gallows and asked for compensation for hanging people.

One of those hanged was a Scandinavian nobleman, Count Nils Gustaf von Schoultz. He led the Americans in an attack near Prescott during the 1837 Rebellion and was hanged at thirty-one years of age and then buried in Kingston. The count was an adventurer who had helped the Poles revolt against the Russians and served in the French Foreign Legion. He is described as a man sensitive to the cause of liberty and the unfair treatment of people, but that didn't apply to the wife and two children he abandoned. Von Schoultz was hoodwinked by the Americans into believing that Canadians had been enslaved by the British government and wanted to be liberated. On his way to the gallows he realized he was mistaken about what was happening in the minds of Canadians. The future prime minister of Canada, John A. Macdonald, advised him as a lawyer and got his sentence changed from hanging at the common gallows in Kingston, like his followers, to hanging at a better gallows built for him at the fort. Macdonald was more successful in helping others accused of being rebels and won a lawsuit for the jailor unjustly accused of helping rebels escape from Fort Henry.

Fifteen of the rebels imprisoned in the fort escaped after digging their way out. The men dug for six days with a piece of metal and a nail, and made their way through an underground passageway using a lantern made out of a coffee pot. Two were recaptured and the remaining thirteen made it across the river to Cape Vincent, on the U.S. side.

The fort was left to crumble after 1890, then restored and used during the First World War for more prisoners. This time it was German prisoners of war, spies for the enemy, and people who were just plain suspicious. As many as four hundred people were kept here at one time. The fort was then closed again and reopened as a museum in 1938, on the eve of the Second World War. Once again it was used as a prison. And so it happened that German soldiers became prisoners behind the walls of a Canadian museum. Like their counterparts in the 1837 Rebellion, some of them escaped from the fort. One time nineteen of them crawled out the latrine drain and under the stone walls.

ROYAL MILITARY COLLEGE
(1876)

The college hasn't been glamorized as much as West Point and isn't as well known even in Canada. Still, in a quieter way, it is a source of pride for its graduates, who have gone on to make contributions to Canada and the world. For instance, one of the graduates from the engineering school was Percy Girouard, a French-Canadian who served with the British army in the fight for the Sudan in the late 1890s and later in the Boer War. He masterminded the construction of railways that made the movement of troops and supplies possible over large distances. Other engineering graduates played key roles in the construction of the railways that bound Canada together as a nation.

The college was established in 1876 on the grounds where the British built fortifications and a navy base almost a century before. Navy ships were built here for the inland seas of the Great Lakes. Later, some of the navy buildings were simply converted into the college, which was a better fate for them than the warships that were left to rot. The limestone used for the Mackenzie Building was quarried by convicts from the Kingston Penitentiary, who also made the furniture.

The college was created after the British politicians decided they didn't like the cost of paying for an army in Canada. That meant that Canada had to find a way to train officers for itself. And that was fine, as far as Canada was concerned. The Liberal government under Alexander Mackenzie wanted more independence and it got to spend money lavishly in an old Tory stronghold. In 1876, the college opened a building originally built in 1820 and called the Stone Frigate. According to a story (which isn't true but explains the name), the Stone Frigate was built with money sent from Great Britain to construct a warship. The college has a small museum open in the summertime in one of the Martello defence towers built in 1846. Visitors can also wander around the college grounds, which have buildings dating from the early 1800s. The old stone guardhouse and gate date from 1816 and with the wall were partly intended to keep the townspeople from building shanties on navy ground. The parking lot is one of the best spots to photograph the skyline of Kingston, which lies across the water to the west. The guards in the guardhouse at the old stone wall are friendly and will give directions.

THE KINGSTON PENITENTIARY

(1834)

A THOROUGHLY MODERN PRISON

The great days for touring the Kingston Penitentiary were during the time of Queen Victoria, who reigned from 1837 to 1901. For a fee, the Victorians took their families through the prison to learn how misery and hard work could be used to make people — particularly the Irish — more civilized. Then, as now, prisons were a way of measuring the humanity of a society, and Canadians were proud of the Kingston Penitentiary. They thought it "struck a happy medium between the severity of the Old Country prisons and the laxity of American Institutions." The people of Kingston also thought that the building was the most magnificent in town, after the city hall, of course. One of those drawn here by his interest in prisons was Charles Dickens. Coming at a time of penal reform, Dickens was enthusiastic about the place and the way it was run. After all, in England, a truly nautical nation, the prisoners were put in the hulls of derelict ships. The reservations that Dickens had about the prison in Kingston he kept to himself.[3]

At the time of Dickens's visit, in 1842, there were about two hundred prisoners. Most of the prisoners were thieves, with a smattering of murderers. They came from all parts of society. A few them were women. Some were children, such as the eight-year-old boy sentenced for three years for picking a man's pocket on a steamboat. A number of the convicts were political prisoners. They were caught during the Fenian raids or the rebellion in Upper Canada in 1837.

In 1867, the prison population reached the high for the century of almost nine hundred. By coincidence, that was the year that Canada became a separate nation and could start calling the jail a federal penitentiary. The Kingston Penitentiary was the first national prison in Canada and some of the most distinguished citizens of the city were wardens. Two of the mayors of Kingston ran the prison. It was that kind of town.

The convicts spent their nights in dark cells slightly wider than their metal beds and were given a Bible to read by the dim light of a lantern from the hall. They were kept in silence and solitude so that, like monks, they could meditate on their situation in life. Getting out of prison was so much like a resurrection that it was called the afterlife. The prisoners were flogged if they didn't obey the prison rules. The more rebellious prisoners were put in a stone or wooden coffin with breathing holes. That was intended to make an impression on them. The final arbiter was a device built in the 1850s which locked the head of the convict into a small wooden barrel. Icy water was poured into the barrel from above. The water drained slowly from the space around the neck. It gave terrific headaches. The sightseers learned all this and often followed a visit by writing down their best ideas on ways to reform people who weren't as virtuous as themselves.

Under the first warden, Henry Smith, the conditions in the prison alarmed the government. It wasn't as advanced as was thought. The prison had a dark side. A commission of inquiry was called in 1848 to look into, among other things, the mismanagement and cruelty by the warden. By this time, some prisoners were stealing mash from the hogs. Others went mad, including a twelve-year-old boy who became delirious one night and was flogged by the warden. The boy's two brothers were in the prison and one of them, Narcisse, was beaten by the warden with a rope and sent to the Lower Canada Lunatic Asylum. The warden, obviously, wasn't a saint. He was removed after the inquiry but not punished. Eventually, the authorities realized that not everybody in the prison was a criminal. Some, they thought, were insane. So they converted a mansion on the waterfront, called Rockwood, into an asylum. The criminals were separated from the insane, and the insane — another type of lawbreaker — put into their own prison.

The prisoners of the time were citizens of the Industrial Revolution. Idleness was thought to lead to immorality and crime, and so a prison like this one was a kind of factory. Private companies contracted to have the prisoners work for them, the prisoners' pay going towards the cost of the penitentiary. Starting in the 1840s, they turned out vast numbers of things. They worked as masons, carpenters, tailors and shoemakers. The prisoners were particularly good at making furniture. Some of it was carved and so exotic it would have been worth stealing. The prisoners made the original red uniforms for the North-West Mounted Police, as well as the Mounties' shirts, socks, and boots. They also made locks to keep homes safe from criminals like themselves. They had a foundry for casting iron and the prison was industrialized with steam engines. Some of what they made was loaded onto ships at the prison wharf and sent to other parts of the country.

The prison was built at Hatter's Bay starting about 1834, and a decade later the convicts built limestone walls and a gatehouse, using rock quarried inside the walls. Like much of Kingston, the prison was originally a waterfront facility that relied on ships to bring supplies. The convicts could see the masts of the ships coming and going along the edge of the walls. The prison had a steam yacht for the warden. The boat was named after the vengeful goddess Juno, who had the eyes of an ox. One time, when the ox wasn't looking, two convicts escaped on the warden's yacht.

The regular tours of the prison stopped in 1911 because they invaded the privacy of the convicts. They turned the prisoners into creatures living in a kind of goldfish bowl. The stream of visitors also made it impossible to control the smuggling. A small but exotic museum across the street from the prison is open during the summertime. It has everything from weapons made by the convicts to a painting that an inmate did of the Madonna.

BARRIEFIELD

Situated on a limestone cliff overlooking Kingston and the Cataraqui River, Barriefield was once a complete community unto itself. It could be cold here, exposed to the winds in the wintertime, but wonderful in the summertime, when the tiny community got a cool breeze and had none of the bugs and swamps that bothered the poor souls below. There are still old limestone homes here and walking through the streets can give you a sense of what life might have felt like in the mid-1800s.

One of the sights to see in Barriefield is St. Mark's Church (1843), built by people associated with the old British navy shipyard. It was initially proposed that the church be located inside the walls of one of the forts, but that never happened. For one hundred years, the bell used in this church was from the old British navy shipyard.

In the 1930s and 1940s, one of the few real folk heroes of Kingston, a bootlegger known as Dollar Bill, lived in Barriefield. He sold booze at tables inside a seaplane hangar on the waterfront and he was loved by the community because of his generosity to kids and adults. His gruffer side came out if he didn't want to serve a customer. He'd fire his shotgun in the air and yell, "Get out of here, you cockroaches." The bootlegger was caught and fined several times, but the people of the community, including, it's said, a few police officers, usually kept him warned of raids.

✦ OTHER ATTRACTIONS ✦

Queen's University
Agnes Etherington Art Centre
Murney Tower Museum
Bellevue House
Pump House Steam Museum
Canadian Forces Communications and Electronics Museum
Princess of Wales Own Regiment Military Museum
International Ice Hockey Federation Museum
Kingston Archaeological Centre
MacLachlan Woodworking Museum on Highway 2 east of
    Kingston

Farmer George Eves on Simcoe Island between Wolfe Island and Kingston.

WOLFE ISLAND

WOLFE ISLAND FERRY

I T WOULDN'T FEEL LIKE Kingston if there weren't a ferry travelling back and forth every day between the city and Wolfe Island. It's like knowing that the sun will rise again tomorrow. A ferry has been making the trip, in different forms, since the days of the early settlers on the island in the 1800s. And now, with regular service, people keep track of the ferry, unconsciously, as it runs, whatever the weather, with the regularity of a clock.

The first ferries to Wolfe Island were propelled by wind and sails and oars. As the ferries grew in size and acquired steam engines, they became an even more important link to Kingston and the mainland. That link prolonged the existence of farming on Wolfe Island years after it had died out on other islands because of problems of transportation and economics.

The ferry service wasn't always as reliable as it is today, now that the difficulties of fog and ice have more or less been solved. In the early 1900s, the ferry navigated through snow and fog by a compass and stopwatch. That wasn't easy, because a vein of iron running across the harbour could draw the compass off by ten degrees and the metal of the cars confused it. The ferry service also had to stop in the wintertime because of ice on the river. The problem of navigating in ice was solved in the 1970s when five kilometres of pipe was laid along the bottom of the river. The pipe has holes in it and air is pumped through the pipe to make bubbles. The bubbles stir up the warmer water on the bottom and help keep the channel clear of ice for the ferry.

The Wolfe Island ferry, run by the province since 1964, is a good way to see the river and the island. Some people leave their cars on the mainland and board the ferry just for the pleasure of the ride. Others take their cars to tour the island and cross to the American side of the river by the small ferry on the south side of the island.

THE ICE BRIDGE

For hundreds of years, the ice that froze on the river in the wintertime was a blessing for the communities on the islands. It helped them to survive and seemed to compensate for suffering the wind and rough water through the rest of the year. The ice joined the communities of both countries on the river by forming a bridge from Kingston to Wolfe Island to Cape Vincent. The islanders marked the path across the ice with evergreen branches and found all sorts of ingenious ways to cross it. They skated, and sailed on iceboats, and raced horses that had been specially shod for ice. It gave them a sense of freedom and exhilaration.

When the ice was forming or breaking up, travel was more difficult. Neither boats nor sleighs would work, so the islanders used iceboats that ran across the ice on metal runners and floated across the patches of open water. As the engines improved, the people started using metal boats that were pushed across either ice or water by an aircraft engine mounted at the back.

Historically, the ice was one of the forces that shaped the area. It was used as a route by smugglers and by convicts escaping from the penitentiary in Kingston. It also made the area vulnerable to attacks from across the border. During the Rebellion of 1837, the Americans planned an invasion that would move across the ice from French Creek. The commander of the fort at Kingston at the time was prepared for that. He protected Kingston by ordering that holes be chopped in the ice. Deserters also used the frozen river as a way to escape the British army. That worked until March, when the ice started to break up. Then the desperation of the deserters increased, as did their numbers, and the cannon boomed to tell everyone in earshot that they were missing. A detachment of soldiers was stationed on Wolfe Island to try to catch the deserters before they made it across the border. There's a story of one deserter during the War of 1812 who escaped across the ice. His legs were badly frozen and eventually both feet had to be amputated.

In the late 1930s, one of the most famous creatures on the ice was a twenty-one-year-old mare named Minnie. The horse lived on Wolfe Island and was sent across the ice on her own, pulling a sleigh loaded with either farm produce for Kingston or provisions for the island. Minnie was a small, tough, hardworking mustang from out west — "the contrariest thing that ever had four feet," according to one islander — and was owned by a smug- gler. The horse had uncanny knack for sensing bad ice. She'd stop and go around a weak spot before anyone else could see it.

Ice being ice, it broke at times, plunging people and animals into the cold water. It may sound heartless now, but old and weak animals were once used to test for bad ice. Since the horses were positioned ahead of the sleigh, they fell in first. If they fell through and drowned, that proved that the ice was bad. The drivers tied an extra piece of rope around their necks — a kind of choke rope — in case this happened. With a yank from the rope, the horse became a kind of inflated bag of wind. The full technique for hauling the horse out was to push it deeper into the water. The horse started paddling furiously and shot up in a rush. At the same time as the animal was rising, the men shoved a plank under it and heaved it out onto solid ice. On one trip, Minnie the Mare, a veteran of the technique, had to be pulled out five times.

But not every horse was so lucky. One time a horse and a sleigh loaded with seventeen people, including young children, crashed through the ice. The people survived, but the horse went to the bottom of the river with the sleigh. There were others who had accidents, such as the future prime minister of Canada, Alexander Mackenzie. He fell through the ice twice while an employee of a quarry on the island, cutting stone for the Welland Canal. He saved himself with a long pole he carried.

Drownings have also occurred in recent years as a result of people driving cars and snowmobiles across the frozen river. In the 1940s, the owner of a grocery store on Wolfe Island broke through the ice and sank to the bottom of the river in his truck. When he was found he was still behind the steering wheel. A particularly tragic drowning happened in 1984, when a mother and her two children plunged through the ice in their car. After that, the city of Kingston passed a bylaw to prevent people from entering the municipality across the ice.

Islanders follow the change of seasons through the coming and going of the ice. In the spring, the ice on the lake and the river breaks up, ending the long winter lull when the waves are silent. Soon the birds start singing and the waves start crashing. The break-up begins when the ice on the river gets softer and assumes a honeycombed structure. Then the ice piles up in layers on the shore. Sometimes these walls of ice are over six feet high. In the past, ice like that could jam the river and cause flooding. Although it sounds like a tall tale today, it is said that the river used to freeze to the bottom.

In Morrisburg one day, in 1887, the water rose four metres above normal due to flooding caused by an ice jam. Across the border a farmer had to build platforms to keep his cattle from drowning. A house nearby was cut down by the ice, and, what the ice didn't demolish, the fire from the stove did. Another time, a brick house on the shore was cut down by the ice and the people inside barely escaped with their lives.

CATHCART REDOUBT

(1847)

The tower on the small island across from Fort Henry was built by the British to defend against attacks by ships in the mid-1800s. The bay beyond the tower is called Deadman Bay. It was named after men working on the tower drowned there one stormy afternoon when their overloaded work-boat sank. Eighteen men died in the water and when others went to look for them, three more drowned.

GARDEN ISLAND

Just before the ferry reaches Wolfe Island, it passes Garden Island, once one of the most industrious places on the river. The island was owned and administered by the Calvin Company, which built ships and assembled timber rafts. At its busiest point in the 1800s, the island was a community of seven hundred. One of the biggest tasks was to assemble the enormous timber rafts to float down the St. Lawrence River and through the rapids. Wooden cabins with bunks and a stove were built on these rafts for the crew. The rafts were propelled by sails and oars, with so many sails that one raft could look like a fleet of ships. Later, the rafts were towed down the river and through the rapids by steamboats. It took about three days to go from Kingston to Montreal. The owner of the Calvin Company said that it might be a wonderful experience to go through the rapids in a passenger steamer, but from a raft "one saw the wild water at close range and felt its power." The rafting stopped at the beginning of the First World War, when the Calvins went to war and the era of the wooden sailing ships came to an end.

D.D. Calvin's company employed almost everybody on the island. It built the stores, operated the library, and issued its own paper money. All this, in the words of historian Donald Swainson, was presided over by Calvin as a "benevolent patriarch." Photographs of the man show that he had deep, far-reaching eyes that sat recessed under bushy eyebrows. His eyes appeared as though they were waiting for a future they'd already seen. His young son and heir was killed in the explosion of the boiler on a steamboat called the *Hercules*.

In wintertime, when work on the ships and the rafts ended, the people on the island built ships. One of their finest efforts was the construction of a vessel named the *Garden Island*, which sailed the Atlantic and eventually sank off the coast of Ireland. During the wintertime, when the schooners were locked in the frozen river, they were loaded with blocks of ice cut from the river, to be shipped in the spring to American ports on Lake Erie.

These days the island is the intensely private retreat of cottagers who still rent the land from the company. The bottom of the bay on the protected east side is littered with the pieces of old ships that were built there.

WOLFE ISLAND

The Indians came here first, two thousand years ago, to the biggest island at the upper end of the river, and called the island Ganounkouesnot. Many different groups used the island over the centuries. The Mississauga Ojibwa camped here through the winter, hunting bear, deer and foxes. They even buried their dead here, which is the mark of a true islander.

The French came next. They claimed the island of Ganounkouesnot for themselves without consulting with the Indians. Like other islands in the area, Ganounkouesnot went through a succession of names. In the early 1700s it was called Hog Island because (like the four or five other Hog Islands on the river) some swine were let loose here and multiplied. In 1792, the old island of the Indians and the French was named after James Wolfe, the British general who defeated the French. The name symbolized the change in nationality. Even though the name of the island changed, much of the land was still held by French descendants, such as the Baroness de Longueuil, who had a house on the island.

A freighter passes a farmhouse on Wolfe Island.

Settlers started arriving in the early 1800s. They chose Wolfe Island for the same reasons that others chose nearby islands — the availability of timber and the limestone quarries. Once the land had been cleared, the farmers came looking for cheap land, which they leased. The population of the island swelled in the 1840s and 50s, until it peaked at 3,600 people in the 1860s. Then it went into a steady decline, hitting a stable 1,200 in the 1930s.

In 1852, construction of a canal across the island was started. The idea was to make Kingston an important railway link to the United States. The mouth of the river was too exposed to the wind and the waves coming off Lake Ontario, and so a canal was proposed for barges to carry railway cars. The canal opened in 1857 and closed in 1932. Now it's a good spot for catching fish, trapping muskrats, and hunting ducks. People on the island give directions of places as "above" or "below" the old canal.

The islanders are still as independent today as they were in the 1800s. They have electricity and telephones, but no stop lights. They plow their own roads in the wintertime and have their own fire department and ambulance department run by volunteers. A former reeve of the island says that they don't need a police department: an island where everybody knows everybody else is too small for much delinquency. Apparently, a few years ago a man tried to steal a car on the island. He was chased by the islanders into a dead-end road where his pursuers threw him into a snowbank.

HORNE FERRY

One of the most charming rides across the river — although it's short — is on the small Horne ferry. The ferry service between Cape Vincent, on the U.S. side, and Wolfe Island on the Canadian side, started with one row boat in the early 1800s. It became an official, private, family-operated business in 1829, with a lease from King George IV of England. It passed into the Horne family when the daughter of the original operator married a Horne in the 1900s.

The ferry service has always been considered essential. During the War of 1812, people working on ferries were exempt from the militia in Canada. The Horne ferry has had its historical moments. It was seized and held briefly by Americans during the 1837 Rebellion to prevent the British from learning about their planned invasion of Prescott. That disastrous invasion became known as the Battle of the Windmill. The ferry was also used to expel suspicious characters from Canada during the 1837 Rebellion.

❧ OTHER ATTRACTIONS ❧

Sacred Heart of the Blessed Virgin Mary Roman Catholic Church (1916–1917)

The Cape Vincent French Festival.

CAPE VINCENT

NAPOLEONIC ASPIRATIONS

I T'S FUNNY HOW a person's popularity can grow even after death. That's what happened with Napoleon Bonaparte in the Thousand Islands in the 1800s. In Europe, Napoleon was known as a big troublemaker and was not well liked by the British. The last thing they did to him was to send him into exile on an island full of rats. And yet the Americans, who had rebelled from the British, were fond of Napoleon. Along the southern shore of the St. Lawrence River, parents gave the name Napoleon to their children. There were lots of little Napoleons running around.

Napoleon's connection with Cape Vincent has been celebrated for years, particularly since the village is one of the last reminders of the French presence in the Thousand Islands. Except for this community, most traces of the French, ultimately defeated by the British in Canada in 1759, have been obliterated at the upper end of the river. After the French were defeated in Canada, the American Revolution, supported by the French, allowed the French a degree of revenge. Then, in the 1820s, after the defeat of Napoleon by the British, a few French settlers founded Cape Vincent at the head of the river.

According to a book published in 1906, and still the main source of history in the village today,[4] the members of the French colony planned to rescue Napoleon from his prison on St. Helena and make a refuge for him

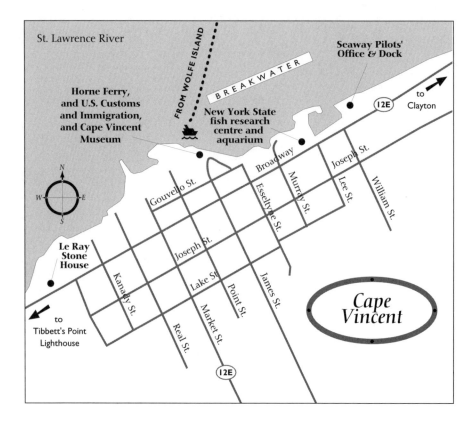

in the village. It's true that Napoleon, on his island prison, dreamt of coming to the United States and of rousing the French in Canada against the British. And so, when his brother Joseph bought property near the border at Cape Vincent, there was fear that a colony there would contaminate the area and attract French–Canadians hostile to the British. Napoleon believed that Canada would inevitably be absorbed by the United States, but then, if you asked him, he also thought that he could conquer the world. That was one more dream that wasn't fulfilled.

Some people in Cape Vincent believe that a house in the community was built for Napoleon. That's unlikely, although the house did belong to Napoleon's chief of police, a blustery man named Pierre Francois Réal.

There was a room in the house devoted to Napoleon, with some of the emperor's possessions. Among the possessions was a painting of one of Napoleon's favourite authors, the philosopher Jean-Jacques Rousseau. Napoleon, it seems, was a bit of a bookworm. Napoleon's belongings in the house in Cape Vincent were stolen when the building burned down in 1867. By coincidence, this is also the year that Canada became a separate nation, neither Napoleonic nor British.

The choice of Cape Vincent and the Thousand Islands would ultimately have been a galling one for Napoleon, had he ever escaped from St. Helena and decided to live in such a remote spot. Here the British named some of the islands after the ships and commanders who fought against him. Wellesley Island, for instance, was named after Arthur Wellesley, the Duke of Wellington, who defeated Napoleon at Waterloo. The body of water between Wellesley Island and Hill Island was at one time called Lake Waterloo. But among the islands there was also a St. Helena, recalling the place of Napoleon's imprisonment. Even the name Cape Vincent recalls, by coincidence, the terrible defeat of France's ally Spain in 1797 at Cape St. Vincent off Portugal. That defeat, in turn, prevented the French from invading Britain. Imagine Napoleon trying to escape to a place guaranteed to remind him of what went wrong in his life.

Cape Vincent was named after the Frenchman Vincent LeRay, Comte de Chaumont, who sold part of his family's land to a small colony of Napoleonic exiles. When Napoleon's circle lost its influence with the fall of Napoleon, it's true that some of them came here. However, it is also said that Napoleon's sister Caroline and his brother Joseph, once the King of Spain, lived in the Cape. Unfortunately, that's not true. The former king lived near Philadelphia, which had much more wealth and power than he would find on the frontier at Cape Vincent. Joseph may have visited his associates in the Cape from time to time.

Napoleon died in 1821. Cape Vincent grew without him, losing whatever command of the French language it once had. Today, the community has an elaborate French festival every year on a weekend close to July 14, Bastille Day. Whatever happened to all these French people? As one villager says, "They just all died off."

In the years that followed the French initiative, Cape Vincent became an important port at the head of the river and established a shipbuilding industry. The port was so important that in 1860 a thousand ships stopped here. Commercial fishermen and cheese factories relied on the ships for access to the markets of the cities.

One of the largest fishing operations in the area in the 1920s was run by Captain Claude Cole, who owned the Duck Islands in Lake Ontario. His nickname was King Cole and, according to the story, he tried to raise buffalo and angora goats on the Duck Islands. Cole later became a smuggler, using his fishing operation on the Duck Islands as a base. He died of a heart attack while driving on a fish company dock. If his car hadn't hit a post, he would have died in the water.

In 1818, a customs house was established in Cape Vincent with a ferry running between the village and Kingston. During Prohibition, the community had a station for the United States Border Patrol. However, it also served as a home to smugglers and was prey to all kinds of invaders. Part of the folklore of the town is that Canadians used to cross the ice and steal bodies out of the graveyard. They apparently needed bodies for anatomy lessons at medical school.

The village of Cape Vincent was incorporated in 1853, a year after the railway arrived to connect with the port and bolster the transportation network. At that time Cape Vincent had over 1,200 people.

CAPE VINCENT MUSEUM
(CIRCA 1830)

Just beside the ferry dock is a stone barracks that was built for soldiers during the War of 1812. Although the Cape lay in an exposed position and the people felt vulnerable to all sorts of raids from Canada, it didn't have a fort to make it a military target and so was largely unscathed by the war. The worst incident it can claim was a minor British attack that left three people dead. The community was also raided during the war by two soldiers in a canoe. The British soldiers convinced the American officers that they were part of a larger invasion force and took them prisoner. After the war, the barracks became a foundry where cast iron stoves and ironwork for ships were made.

During the 1837 Rebellion, there were rumours that Canadians intended to cross the ice and attack the village. They were exposed on the border, and with so many people passing through the village there was always a lot of wild speculation. The villagers might also have felt a twinge of fear as there were sympathizers to the rebellion among them. The leader of these sympathizers, William Lyon Mackenzie, escaped across the border disguised as a woman. He was rumoured to have taken shelter in a home in the village. With the rumour of the attack, the women — and perhaps Mackenzie in disguise — were taken out of the village to safety. A school teacher from the village was taken prisoner at the Battle of the Windmill and — no rumour this time — hanged in Kingston.

L E R A Y   S T O N E   H O U S E
(1 8 1 5)

This summer home made of limestone is typical of Cape Vincent but not of other villages on this side of the border. It was built for the wealthy and influential LeRay family. The building was called the Stone House from the beginning because it was the first stone home built in the town. The limestone came from a quarry on Carleton Island, which was once also the location of key British fortifications on the river.

OLD RAILWAY STATION (1853)

A marina on the waterfront was once the Cape Vincent railway station. The rail line into the village, constructed in 1852, was built, accidentally, through an old Indian burial ground. The rail line operated for almost one hundred years. At one time attached to the railway station, was a hotel, but it was demolished by a hurricane in 1887.

The rail brought visitors in and took goods out. These goods included hay to feed racehorses and fish, caught in Lake Ontario, to feed the people of New York City. Thick, clear, black ice, cut out of the lake, was also sent by rail to New York City. As a local resident says, because of the ice and cold winters, "A lot of people think we freeze up here." The residents of Cape Vincent, however, learned to enjoy the cold winters. In the days when the river froze solid, ice boats rigged with sails raced along the waterfront.

PILOTS' STATION

One of the oldest professions on the river is that of the river pilot. For hundreds of years, pilots have been guiding ships and timber rafts past the shoals, through the twists and turns in the channels of the Thousand Islands, and then over the rapids further down the river. The construction of the St. Lawrence Seaway in the 1950s put an end to the bumpy ride on the rapids. At the same time, the seaway brought larger ships. Today, all foreign ocean-going vessels are still required to have a local pilot on board. On any given day you can see at least four or five freighters flying flags from countries as far away as Greece, Norway, Liberia and Japan. About three thousand freighters a year use the seaway. Depending on a ship's direction, the river pilots either board at Cape Vincent or leave it here.

Pilots say that this is the most difficult river in the world for ocean vessels to navigate. The pilots are under terrific pressure, having to work with foreign crews and unfamiliar equipment. There are a great number of near misses, and the occasional collision or grounding. "You gotta watch for that early mornin' fog," says one old sailor. "You got them bays with swamps just below the Thousand Islands bridge and the fog just rolls in." But it's all good fun for the pilots and some of them work until they're seventy years old.

Pilots must contend with a number of conditions in the river. There is no tide, but there is a strong current flowing to the sea. At the narrow points of the river, the current goes as fast as two knots. The pilots must compensate for the speed of the current and the force of the wind blowing against the ship. The biggest freighters are two hundred and twenty-two metres long. These freighters must pass each other in channels as narrow as ninety metres. The pilots also have to watch their speed very carefully. The river, like a highway, has speed limits. River police use a radar gun and any vessels caught speeding get a speeding ticket.

FISHERIES RESEARCH STATION & AQUARIUM
(1856)

New York State operates a fisheries research station in what was once a steam-powered grist mill. In 1895, the state bought the building and turned it into a fish hatchery. The eggs are hatched in glass jars inside the building.

An aquarium in the basement of the building is open to the public. Here you can come face to face with the fish of the river, including the longnosed gar, with a snout like Pinocchio. The eggs of this fish are toxic to human beings, but its flesh is quite edible. It has never been a popular fish, though, either to catch or to eat.

TIBBETT'S POINT ROAD

This coastal road to the lighthouse offers one of the best views of the river, which is why it was useful for smugglers during Prohibition. One time a man from Gananoque saw smugglers unloading here. He noticed that they were making an awful racket. "Aren't you worried about the sheriff," he asked one man. The man replied, "I am the sheriff."

The road has some of the oldest limestone homes in the area. The homes were built in the early 1800s by the French, including some from the Napoleonic circle. The homes were made out of limestone, which was not the material of preference for the Yankees. Canadians built their structures using granite, limestone and brick, but Americans preferred wood. The exceptions on the United States side are the churches and the homes of wealthy islanders. The first French landowner, de Chaumont, would have felt welcome in the area since his name comes from the French word for limestone.

TIBBETT'S POINT LIGHTHOUSE
(1854)

There's a good wide view of the open water at the head of the St. Lawrence River from the lighthouse, which is one of six along the main shipping channel from Cape Vincent to Ogdensburg. The first lighthouse, built here in 1827 on land that belonged to Captain John Tibbett, burned whale oil. The lighthouse is now automated.

GRENADIER ISLAND

In 1813, an American armada of three hundred boats, intent on invading Canada at Montreal, made a camp at Grenadier Island, near Cape Vincent. Not only was the armada no secret to the British, partly because of information from the island, but a bad storm on the river turned out to be more hazardous than the commanders anticipated. Many of the boats were wrecked. Meanwhile, during the same gale, a Scotsman, Lieutenant-Colonel Red George Macdonell, led a British flotilla from Kingston down the river and through the rapids to meet the Americans. After more

*T*he wreck of a scow at Grenadier Island.

trouble, the American flotilla was led through the islands by the renegade William Johnston but ran into difficulty. In the end there was the disastrous routing of the Americans at the Battle of Crysler's farm. The officer in charge, Major General James Wilkinson, had once served under Benedict Arnold and had a career strewn with conspiracies. After the Battle of Crysler's farm, he lost his command.

Grenadier Island has the same name as a large island downriver at Rockport, on the Canadian side of the river. The duplication of island names is typical in the area and one of the problems of navigating here. There are so many islands with the same names that it can be confusing even to local people.

CARLETON ISLAND

In the mid–1700s, the British selected Carleton Island, with its high lime-stone cliff on the west, as an ideal place for a fort and navy base. From here, they felt they could control the main channel of the St. Lawrence River along the frontier. The island became a centre for British shipbuilding during the American Revolution. The British warship *Ontario*, with twenty-two guns, was built here. The ship was later lost with all on board during a storm on the Great Lakes.

The island was a refuge for Loyalists and Indian allies such as Molly Brant. It was also a place to launch Indian raids on the Mohawk Valley. As with most military posts near the border, it was a convenient spot for soldiers who wanted to desert. A corporal on the island was once arrested in his bed and given six hundred lashes because his comrades suspected he was thinking about deserting.

With tension between the British and the Americans, the island fort was in a precarious position, and the British needed the Indians. The Indians knew the frontier better than the Americans and the British. The British used them as scouts to protect the fort from what they called insults, or attacks. The Indians also supplied the fort with fresh meat in the wintertime. However, one officer complained that the friendly Indians, who took scalps during raiding parties to the Mohawk Valley, were getting mixed up with the enemy Indians and the British couldn't tell them apart.

The treaty that ended the revolutionary war in 1783 set down the boundary between the two countries. This left the island in the waters of the United States, but the British kept the island for a while nevertheless. At the same time, in 1783-84, the British negotiated a treaty on the island to bamboozle land from the Mississauga Ojibwa. The Indians surrendered the north shore of the river and the lake. At that time the island had a garrison of over seven hundred men and an Indian village of about five hundred people. The British dismantled part of the fort and moved to what later became Kingston.

By 1791, a sergeant and twelve men were left to defend the barracks from the Americans. The British didn't have their heart in the spot. At the beginning of the War of 1812, the army at the fort had dwindled to a sergeant, three invalids, and two women. They were captured by a boatload of Yankees led by Captain Abner Hubbard, the innkeeper from the nearby community of Millen's Bay.

After the British left the island, the settlers and the smugglers thought it would be a comfortable location to settle. It's hard to imagine today that a small island like this one could support an entire community. But, in the early 1800s, three to four hundred people lived on the island. Their main occupation was fishing. In 1823, one of the first schools in the area was built here, as well as another essential service, a tavern. The island was considered one of the nicest spots on the river, with fresh air to cure the ague, and plenty of wild raspberries, strawberries and plums. On nearby islands, the French collected gull eggs to eat.

The monolithic navigation buoys from the shipping channel are stored at Clayton in the wintertime.

CLAYTON

THE BEST SPOONS ON THE RIVER

CLAYTON

THE THOUSAND ISLANDS has changed so much since the mid-1800s that it's hard to imagine how Clayton once looked. In a town created by timber barons and ship captains, ships were part of the architecture and landscape of the town. When the ships were put into the ways for repairs, their prows would hang over the main street. The shipbuilding industry began here following the War of 1812, when a man named William Angel assembled the big rafts of timber at the waterfront. In time, the business expanded to employ three hundred men in a good season. A shipyard opened in 1832 and the business went so well that it alone put about two hundred and fifty men to work. One of the partners, a captain, owned two-thirds of the town. Other captains did equally well as barons of the shipping industry. Schooners were built here for the river and the lakes and even merchants from Kingston came here to have their ships constructed. The town also had a factory for the type of boat named after the river, the St. Lawrence skiff.

In about 1801, a shadowy figured called Captain Bartlett started a ferry from Clayton to Gananoque, tying the two communities together long before the international bridge was built. The river and the ferries kept the two communities close, along with marriages and family ties, although the people still followed their individual inclinations of loyalty or disloyalty to

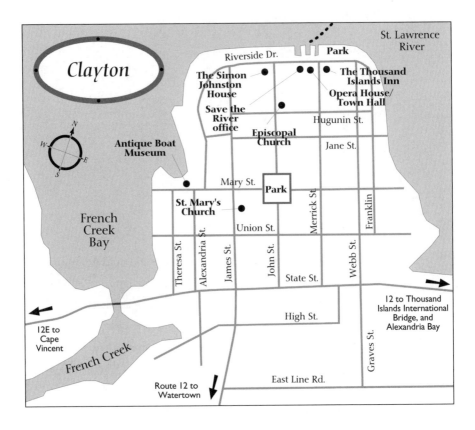

the British Crown. As for Captain Bartlett, according to the story, he beat a hasty retreat from Clayton when he burned his cabin at French Creek. The ferry business probably wasn't enjoyable anyway, since, at that time Captain Bartlett would have had to row his customers across the river. The steamboat made the life of a ferry captain more comfortable.

In the 1870s the railway arrived, relatively late, to link up with steamboats on the river. That increased the flow of visitors through Clayton. The town made the transition to tourism and the rhythms of life were affected accordingly. People wanted to fish and to be taken around the river by boat.

The town has been a base for fishing guides since the late 1800s. Like most ports a century ago, Clayton had some good bars for rafters and sailors, including one called The Bucket of Blood. The shipbuilding industry persisted as late as the Second World War when submarine chasers were built here. Clayton also manufactured the best spoon — or so they say — ever made for catching fish, the Skinner Trolling Spoon.

Clayton has the largest intact old waterfront on the river, mainly due to the stubbornness of the merchants a century ago. A wealthy man offered them money to move across the street to keep the view of the river clear, but they wouldn't budge. The view in town only improves when a building burns down and nobody rushes to put another in its place. It will take a lot more fires to perfect the view of the river, which is still partly glimpsed through the alleyways between the buildings.

Be warned that Clayton is a peninsular town, tricky to navigate, with all the roads in the core of Clayton coming to an end at the water. One advantage of the peninsula is that the winds blow across it and keep it cool and healthy in the summertime. According to local people, the storms, particularly in the winter, blow over Clayton and dump their load downriver on the people of Alexandria Bay. Clayton also has a river tempo, which tends to be either relaxed or lethargic, depending on your point of view. People here say that things get done in their own time and, if nothing else, they get done right. Those who move here from the city can't help making comments like "The minute we hit the river, we slowed down."

FRENCH CREEK

At the western edge of Clayton is French Creek. The name French Creek — now pronounced in English — is representative of what happened to the French culture in the Thousand Islands. The telephone directory of Clayton is filled with the French names of families who don't speak a word of French. French Creek was named for Peter Penet, a Frenchman who came to America to supply arms to the rebellious Yankees during the

American Revolution. Another Frenchman, James LeRay de Chaumont, acquired the land that is now Clayton and divided it up according to his own design. The streets of old Clayton were named after relatives of this Frenchman and the section west of John Street was known as French Town. Reinforcing the French heritage of the community were the Quebec families who settled here with the start of the rafting trade.

The creek was a trade route into the interior. It was also a favourite path for smugglers from the 1800s right up to Prohibition in the 1930s, when loads of booze were hidden among the boats of the fishing guides. During the War of 1812, a British fleet of two brigs, two schooners, and eight gunboats attacked a camp here that was part of the force organized to invade Canada at Montreal. Later, during the 1837 Rebellion, the ill-fated invasion against Gananoque was launched from French Creek, with William Johnston as one of the conspirators. The invasion force crossed the ice to Hickory Island and then dissipated into the wind.

PIRATE JOHNSTON
& CLAYTON

William Johnston crossed the border from Canada and made Clayton his home. Johnston was a merchant in Kingston and was arrested during the War of 1812. He escaped from prison and made trouble in the islands using a barge armed with three-pound guns and powered by twelve oars. There wasn't a prison that could keep him — or a mud bank he didn't hit. Johnston was driven by anger. He waged a one-man war against the British in Canada that eventually stretched between the War of 1812 and the 1837 Rebellion. During the years between the wars, he was involved in piracy throughout the islands. He didn't care who the victims were.

Johnston was appointed commander-in-chief of the naval forces of the Provisional Government of the Republic of Upper Canada, which was about as significant as being made Emperor of the Moon. The republic didn't have a naval force and when Johnston tried to steal a ship, he couldn't run it. An indication of his true sympathies lies in the name he gave to one of his sons: Bonaparte.

Johnston did not fit in anywhere, and so he came to Clayton, which Canadians at the time saw mainly as an asylum for smugglers, deserters, and sympathizers of republican causes. Sought by both the British and American governments, Johnston disappeared into the islands and used them as his base. For a time, the British believed that he and his gang were located at French Creek. He was also said to have a base on Wellesley Island and one or two smaller islands in the area. In an attempt to root him out, the British had a brainstorm. They declared the whole of the islands — largely uninhabited anyway in the 1830s — under martial law. It didn't work, however, because they couldn't find him. It was like trying to catch fog. The islands and the river were a frontier that couldn't be controlled. There wasn't even the space for a good naval battle.

Johnston settled in Clayton between the War of 1812 and the 1837 Rebellion, and, after serving a brief imprisonment in New York State, he returned as the keeper of the Rock Island lighthouse between Clayton and Wellesley Island. He eventually died in Clayton at eighty-eight years of age, which wasn't a bad end for a renegade.

WALKING IN CLAYTON

A quick way to become acquainted with this old river town is by walking along Riverside Drive next to the St. Lawrence River, starting at the Thousand Islands Inn.

Go past the antique opera house with a weather vane in the shape of a muskie (the prime game fish of the river). Then turn south onto John Street, the old dividing line between the French and the English. At the public docks midway along Riverside Drive there is an outdoor gallery of park benches for watching the river. Across the water is Governor's Island.

A freighter passes Clayton.

To the right of Governor's Island is an island called Calumet, with a tower that was part of a castle-like villa that burned down in 1957. Calumet Tower is one of the most recognizable images of Clayton even though it lies outside the town and across the water.

THOUSAND ISLANDS INN
(1896–1897)

The Thousand Islands Inn is one of the last remaining waterfront hotels in the area. Most of the other inns, particularly those on the islands, have burned down. The Thousand Islands Inn was opened in 1898 by a man whose parents, as part of the French influence, named him Napoleon. In the old days, soot from the steamboats wafted over the building. The sounds of the dock workers kept people awake in their rooms, and everybody from Broadway star May Irwin to rum-runners stayed here. Inns like this one lured people into the area and inspired them to build homes on the islands.

OPERA HOUSE
(1903–1904)

The old opera house was designed by Franklin T. Lent, the same American architect who designed elaborate structures such as the bow-shaped clock tower in Gananoque. "Opera house" was a rather elegant name that many small towns in the United States ascribed to such meeting places. The opera house is now a combination of town hall, muskie and duck decoy museum, and summer theatre.

SAVE THE RIVER OFFICE

The office of the environmental group Save The River, next to the opera house, is a good place to pick up gossip about the river community. Save The River was formed in 1978 to prevent the disruption that would be caused to the environment if the shipping season were kept open through the winter. The organization formed around the charismatic leadership of Abbie Hoffman, a 1960s radical who was hiding here from the FBI under the name Barry Freed. The organization bridged the social gap between the wealthy, liberal summer residents and the less wealthy, conservative river people. Because of the group, winter navigation on the river was terminated. Save The River has adopted the emblem of one of the most quirky and reclusive of river birds, the great blue heron.

JOHNSTON HOME
(1880–1882)

At the corner of Riverside and John streets stands the old home of the ship-building captain Simon G. Johnston. From the square tower in the centre, the captain could keep an eye on his fleet of ships being built in Clayton. By walking south on John Street, you'll see a collection of homes typical of the 1800s, with towers that are either square, round, or octagonal. These structures resemble the architecture of the old homes of Gananoque, directly across the river, but the Clayton homes are built of wood instead of stone.

CHRIST CHURCH EPISCOPAL
(1869–1876)

This large church on John Street is full of nautical themes, beginning with its fish-scale shingles. Some of the stained-glass windows inside show angels with anchors on their shields. One window was dedicated in 1910 to sailors who lost their lives on the Great Lakes. Another window says that Christ "taught people out of a ship." A third, with a scene of Christ at the Sea of Galilee, depicts a St. Lawrence sailing skiff and river bass. The pulpit is said to be shaped like the prow of a ship.

The baptismal font, carved from a piece of pink granite, has a cover to keep out the birds. The birds fly through the open windows, perhaps encouraged by the scene in one window of St. Francis with his arms outstretched to the birds. The Broadway star May Irwin donated one of the stained-glass windows in this church in memory of her son.

ST. MARY'S ROMAN CATHOLIC CHURCH
(1885–1889)

This church, in typical Catholic fashion, has obliterated the sense of the world outside with thick stone walls and an austere marble interior. It has none of the local touches found in churches of other denominations along the river. The cornerstone, made out of local pink granite, seems out of place in the massive grey limestone building.

THE ANTIQUE BOAT MUSEUM

Before leaving Clayton, it's a good idea to get steeped in the significance of boats by visiting the Clayton Antique Boat Museum. Boats are a reflection of the way a society lives, just like houses and cathedrals. This museum contains a collection of old wooden river boats built by craftsmen from the Thousand Islands, including one of the emblems of the area, the St. Lawrence skiff. The museum stands on a small piece of land that juts out into the protected part of the bay where the log rafts were assembled. The museum property was once the raft yard. Later, it became a lumber yard and helped give the bay its local name, Sawdust Bay.

❧ OTHER ATTRACTIONS ❧
The Thousand Islands Craft School and Textile Museum

GRINDSTONE ISLAND

The large island visible in the distance from Clayton is Grindstone Island. Since the early 1800s the island has been inhabited by an independent breed of river people. The island once had a thriving farm community and one of the most productive quarries in the area. The roads of many far-away cities were built from paving stones made of the rock of this island.

One of the biggest early landholders on the island was a man from New Hampshire named William Wells. Typical of the people who came to the islands, he had problems with the ambivalent loyalties of the frontier. His father had fought the British during the American Revolution, but William rebelled from the family, and, at nineteen years of age, came to Canada to be a British subject. He became a local timber baron, taking wood from Wellesley Island, which was once called Wells Island after him. He served in the British militia in the War of 1812 and was taken prisoner in his own home by Americans (under Benjamin Forsyth) on a raid across the border. As a final insult, he leased Grindstone Island from the Indians to rent to farmers, but lost his investment when the island became an American possession.

The people of Grindstone Island remained ungovernable. They gave the British the location of William Johnston when he was hiding on the island.

Woods by water.

A cottage at Thousand Island Park, Wellesley Island.

WELLESLEY ISLAND

REBELS AND CONFEDERATES

THOUSAND ISLANDS
INTERNATIONAL BRIDGE

(1937–1938)

I T'S TOO BAD that you can't live on bridges like this one, since it has a terrific view, and underneath it are ducks, fish and wildflowers. The bridge, which stretches from island to island and is painted green to fit into the surroundings, is the best way to get a spectacular view of the river and the islands without leaving your car. It's even more fun to walk across the bridge — of course, that can mean enduring the wind and the vibrations from the big trucks.

To the east of the Canadian span, the bottom of the river drops quickly to a depth of sixty-seven metres, which is larger than the drop at Niagara Falls. The drop is created by the end of the ledge of rock that forms the basin of Lake Ontario. This is the farthest point to which the saltwater sea — called the Champlain Sea — extended almost twelve thousand years ago. The change in the depth of the river is perceptible in the peculiarities of the current, with odd swirls and smooth patches. Because of its strange current, a place just west of the Canadian span of the bridge is called Whirlpool Island.

When the bridge was built in the 1930s, during the hard times of the Depression, many of the local people found work helping to build it. A large portion of the workers were also Mohawks. One worker fell to his death from the bridge. Another worker saved a man's life by catching him as he fell and then sliding down to safety with his elbow hooked around a metal guide wire. That act of heroism left him with a big scar inside his elbow. The bridge was opened in 1938, a few months before the Second World War started.

Before the bridge was built, the economy and social life of the islands was different. The only way across the river was by boat, and that meant that the river people controlled the transportation. The use of boats also meant that a strong bond formed between river folk on both sides of the river and that the islands could exist as self-sufficient isolated communities.

As soon as the bridge was opened, the old pathways and connections across the river started to disintegrate. There was an invasion of strangers and the economy changed. Old communities began to lose their independence. Even the cottagers became more flighty, staying for a few weeks instead of the whole summer. Many islanders believed that the bridge brought negative influences from outside. This was substantiated with the murder of a woman who was passing through. The killer apparently followed her across the bridge by car.

The bridge also created a new location for crossing the border, and so made customs and immigration offices necessary.

WELLESLEY ISLAND

Anybody who likes Victorian architecture and winding roads will like Wellesley Island. You can spend a day getting lost on the island and distracted by its diversities. The island is divided geographically between two townships and socially by the differences between the old island families and the summer folk from the cities. There's also plenty of wildlife on this island. Large numbers of deer roam the island and cross the roads in the spring and late fall.

Settlers came to the island in the early 1800s to farm and to live off the river by trapping and fishing. They operated dairy farms and took their milk to the cheese factories on the island. A dock established on the south shore, where the bridge is now, served as a steamboat stop to pick up fuel wood. The ferry and the cheese factories were located near the present bridge, where the distance across the river is shortest. The road on the island followed the coastline. Across the centre, which was a mixture of swamp and pasture land, there was only one road.

Every once in a while the tranquillity of this island was disturbed. One time a farmer, looking for some missing cows, discovered the camp of Confederate soldiers who were plotting to liberate Confederate prisoners. The soldiers were roasting some cows at the time. They paid for that indiscretion when the farmer snuck away and sounded the alarm. But mainly, Wellesley Island was a peaceful and meditative place. Farmers here were reminded that they were latecomers by the arrowheads they unearthed when they plowed their fields. In the 1870s, the Methodists built a large camp at Thousand Island Park on the west end. The Presbyterians built another for themselves three years later at Westminster Park on the east end. When people from the cities realized the therapeutic value of being immersed in nature, they began to come here for the summers. It seemed that being on the river calmed people down and made them feel better.

In the centre of the island is the so-called Lake of the Isles, formed from the water between Wellesley and Hill Island. The narrow channel between the two islands is used by boaters who want to escape the noise and congestion on the busier channels. Smugglers used the channel for the same reason during Prohibition. The lake freezes in the wintertime and people drive their trucks out onto the ice to fish.

BILL KEPLER, WELLESLEY ISLAND FARMER

Of all the island farmers in the 1800s, the one who epitomizes the wit and enterprise of the breed best was Bill Kepler of Wellesley Island. Kepler was an orphan and, after five years as a sailor, he came to the island to farm. He started with a used plow, a borrowed horse, and one cow that came as a wedding present. His young wife died of complications during the birth of a child, leaving him to care for the infant while he farmed. His grandson tells how this man rocked the cradle of his newborn child with one foot while milking the cow with his hands. It's said that he plowed the fields with the infant strapped to his back. In time, he found a new wife, but his luck varied as he struggled on. At one point his barn burned down with his animals inside.

As his fortunes improved, Bill Kepler, like other island farmers, took on a number of ventures. He sold cemetery lots on the island, built skiffs, and harvested the loose timber floating in the river to build his docks. He operated a ferry on the south shore where the bridge is now. This is also where the steamboat the *Sir Robert Peel* was seized during the 1837 Rebellion, a few years before Kepler was born. Kepler also built and ran one of the hotels in Alexandria Bay.

A certain Bill Kepler story concerns duck hunting. One day, Kepler went to the Lake of the Isles. He attached small live fish by a line to his duck decoys. The idea was to make the wooden figures move and thus fool the ducks. But some of the self-propelled decoys swam away and attracted the attention of other duck hunters. The hunters blasted away at the ducks. No matter how much the hunters fired, the indestructible ducks ignored them and kept moving.

Even the charming old Densmore Church has a Bill Kepler story. Originally built by farmers, the church is typical of the style of buildings in the area with cedar shingles and a round turret for the entrance. Even the pews are round, curving lengthwise across the room. The church was built in about 1896, and, as the islanders say, "There's nothing new in it." Nowadays the summer people use it as a way of preserving their connection to the island. Their children are baptised and married here. When the farmers of the island got together to build it, Bill Kepler would only make a contribution if some kind of concession were made to his quirky sense of humour. He said that he wanted a turret that was round. Nobody could make much sense out of this request. Kepler insisted it was "So's the devil can't corner me."

Kepler died in 1932 at eighty-seven years of age and is buried with his family at a cemetery on the island near the Thousand Islands Bridge.[5]

THE SIR ROBERT PEEL DOCK

On the old, winding, secluded coastal road, a weathered plaque near the bridge marks the spot where William Johnston and his gang came during the 1837 Rebellion in Canada to steal the steamboat *Sir Robert Peel* and rob the passengers. Johnston, as commodore of the navy of the new republic, desperately needed a ship.

The *Sir Robert Peel*, built in Brockville the year before, had a short and flammable history. One day, the *Sir Robert Peel*, with passengers aboard, was falling behind in a race against the Prescott steamer the *Great Britain* so the crew decided to cheat. They threw every combustible substance they could find into the furnace, including some turpentine. The vessel caught fire and the passengers had to be transferred to the rival ship.

The *Sir Robert Peel* had already been used to transport some of the rebels who were taken prisoner during the 1837 Rebellion, including part of the group that later escaped from Fort Henry at Kingston. At the time that Johnston's gang seized the ship, it was carrying passengers and money. There were rumours that it had the payroll for the British troops. That's not likely, but it was carrying six thousand dollars in bank notes. The boat itself should have been the real prize for the renegades. They had already failed in an attack on Gananoque across the ice and thought it would be easier to take men across the river if they had their own boat. Johnston had a base nearby. He called the base Fort Wallace to give it some inflated grandeur. Unfortunately, for those raiding the steamboat, some of their group got lost. The rest, disguised as Indians, captured the steamboat, but soon realized they didn't know how to run it. Johnston, as commander-in-chief of the navy of the Provisional Government of the Republic of Upper Canada, ran the steamboat onto a mud bank and the rebels had to abandon it. The only option left was to burn and sink the steamboat. Burning ships was a military tactic of the time. The British had already used it on a rebel steamboat. In the end, the biggest threat from the fire was that it would politically inflame the two sides of the border and start a conflict.

Years later, construction workers building the bridge near the Peel Dock thought they saw the shadow of the old steamboat in the river. Divers came to the spot because of rumours that there was $150,000 in gold on the ship. However, nothing was found. Later, a charred wreck, believed to be the *Sir Robert Peel*, was located near the bridge in forty-two metres of water.

These days, the brush has grown back where there once were farms along the Peel Dock Road. The road is good for anybody who's not in a hurry to get somewhere. Driving under the immense bridge is an experience in itself, like being on the underside of the world.

THE EAST END

The road to the east leads through a maze of homes built in the midst of marinas and golf courses. The road has some of the biggest and oldest homes on the island, which, unfortunately, are obscured by the trees.

East of the Densmore Church is the old school house, built in 1890 and now used as a fire hall. The eastern end of the island once had a large hotel and polo fields during the days of the castle builder George Boldt. Most of the hotels on the island have burned down over the years, and the east end is now a patchwork of golf courses where ducks and geese inhabit the water holes during the migration season.

THE WEST END

To the west is a mixture of old farm houses and the elaborate cottages of the summer folk. The first community on the road is Fineview, which, years ago, was an area that offered some relief from the strict Methodist rules of Thousand Island Park farther along. Fineview was once the centre of a farming community that straggled along the road like cows outside a fence. There's a cottage here where Abbie Hoffman went into hiding while a fugitive from the FBI in the 1970s. Hoffman could look out from the cottage and see the lighthouse where William Johnston stayed a century before him. The Fineview Methodist Church, was built here in 1908 with curved pews. The pews were built the same way as skiffs, by softening the wood in steam and bending it in a long curve. As one islander says, "I like these much better. They fit your back." This is the only church on the island with a year-round congregation. The hall in the back is where the islanders vote during elections and, in the wintertime, it's the main meeting hall of the community.

Some of the islanders were raised in homes at this end of the island and trapped along the shoreline. One family was in such a low spot here that their home was flooded regularly in the springtime. They wore rubber boots and the water snakes got into the springs of the beds. The early residents were mainly Methodist, although now the population is more diverse. In 1895, a Hindu swami came to the island and started a retreat that has been continued over the years by other swamis.

Past Fineview, at the tip of the island, is the private community of Thousand Island Park, which brought together the odd mixture on the island of independent, isolated farmers, and rich, cosmopolitan and somewhat fanciful summer residents. These days Thousand Island Park still operates as a complete community, with its own library, post office, museum and churches. The island fireboat is kept here.

The old Methodist cottage community is a kind of gigantic outdoor museum of cottage styles from Victorian times. A large pavilion built over the water once served as the steamboat depot for the summer residents and as the customs office. There was even a ferry powered by horses on a treadmill. From the pavilion and the coastal road you can see the Rock Island Lighthouse where the renegade William Johnston served as keeper after he was pardoned. A lighthouse was a fitting post for the former commander-in-chief of the navy of the Provisional Government of the Republic of Upper Canada who was notorious for hitting mud banks. The lighthouse was built in 1882.

Most of the cottages at the west end of the island in Thousand Island Park are over a century old. The cottages of the wealthy middle class are mini castles with turrets and wide, sweeping porches, probably influenced by the architecture of the two large castles on the river. Some of the old windmills that pumped water from the river are still standing on top of the docks and boathouses.

☙ OTHER ATTRACTIONS ❧

The Tabernacle
The Wellesley Island Hotel and Museum
The Minna Anthony Common Nature Centre

HILL ISLAND

The history of Hill Island is typical for the Thousand Islands area. In the early 1800s, the island was bought for its timber by a man named Billa Larue, and although the present name of the island came from a commander of the armies that fought Napoleon, it was known by the local people for ages as Larue Island. Larue cut the trees and floated the timber down the river in huge rafts.

In the early 1800s, a gang of horse thieves regularly smuggled their contraband across from the mainland to Hill Island. They cut a path across the island to Lake of the Isles and swam the horses across to the American island of Wellesley. The thieves were ambushed one night while crossing the river. One of them was killed and another shot through the jaw.

The Hunts were one of the families that farmed on this island. They came as squatters in the 1850s, and were glad to have the poor, rocky, swampland that nobody else would touch. The arrival of the summer residents created a market in the area for their produce. The Hunts worked hard and were able to make a good living, raising dairy cattle, growing vegetables, and keeping bees. Like the smartest of the island farmers, the Hunts also made money by building a fishing lodge. Farming on the island ended, more or less, with the death of Henry Hiet Hunt Jr., a few days before the official opening of the Thousand Islands bridge in 1938.

FIDDLER'S ELBOW

The name of this channel comes from the old blind fiddler who, years ago, sat at the end of an island here and played his instrument. He lost his eyesight when he was a boy and, according to his elderly grandson, "could see just a shade of ya, but couldn't tell who you was." He died in a weird accident when another boat cut through his skiff and he was impaled by one of his own oars.

A combination cottage and boathouse on an island near Alexandria Bay.

ALEXANDRIA BAY

A TOWN THAT SETS ITS OWN PACE

ALEXANDRIA BAY

THE ONLY THING that makes Alexandria Bay comfortable is living here long enough to stop noticing how odd it is. Nothing in the area of town near the river is straight or level. The rock underneath simply won't allow it. The buildings look like they were put up by mountain goats and the streets are a maze of twists, turns, drops and dead ends.

Alexandria Bay was not built here because it was the best spot for a town; it was simply a convenient place for a supply station. It was named after the son of a French land speculator who, having made a deal to settle some Quakers, saw the need for such a supply station. The first buildings were the tavern and a warehouse that he owned. A community grew up after the War of 1812 and has depended heavily on the river ever since.

In the 1840s, Alexandria Bay had hotels that catered to the fishing gentry. In those days the men wore suits and ties when they went fishing and their skiffs were towed in a group to the fishing grounds by a small steam launch. Sometimes a banjo player would pluck a tune from the roof of the steam launch while the fishermen dined on their catch on the shore.

By the 1870s, big steamboats were stopping here and bringing visitors to stay at the large hotels. In the mid-1870s, a visionary named Elisha Visger started the long, wandering, island boat tours. They would eventually bloom into exotic night cruises of the islands with searchlights picking out

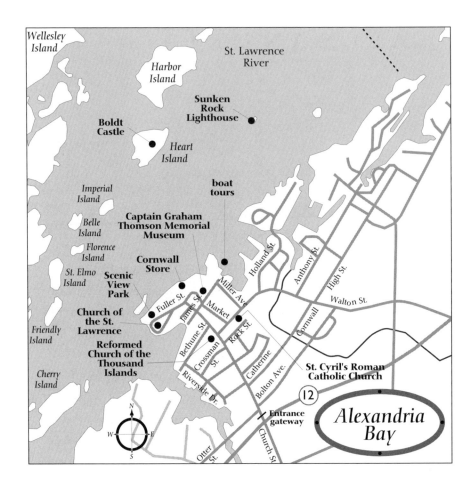

the points of interest. Visger claimed that you got a longer ride than with his competitors and saw more islands on his steamboat, the *New Island Wanderer*. He was credited with "founding" the Lost Channel, where a boatload of soldiers had disappeared in 1760 during the Seven Years' War. By the late 1800s, a flock of hotels and restaurants had sprung up on the islands nearby.

In the 1900s Alexandria Bay continued to be a home for anglers from the cities. These people liked the fishing so much that they built summer lodges and then hotels. The wealthier people built more and more elaborate summer homes on the islands, which reached a pinnacle in Jorstadt Castle and Boldt Castle. Boldt Castle is visible from Alexandria Bay.

Everything went reasonably well in town until the stock market crash of 1929 and the Depression. There was now less money for summer visitors to spend in the area. The local people had to wait for the proliferation of the automobile to see a recovery. Then, with better cars and roads, the middle class came to the islands. After the Second World War there was another slump in tourism, followed by a renaissance in the 1950s. Once again, people wanted to beat the heat and take their families out of the cities. It felt good to enjoy the freedom of the river.

Oddly enough, the railway, which affected the fortunes of so many towns along the river, ignored Alexandria Bay. The rail line only came as far as Redwood, which was then an industrial centre with a glassworks factory. A trolley brought people from Redwood into Alexandria Bay.

THE WATERFRONT

The waterfront of Alexandria Bay is the essence of the town. Many of the services are located on the outer rim and shoreline of the community, with the houses in the centre. This makes it easy to find anything in Alexandria Bay by boat. However, if you come by car, you'll have to crawl along a tangle of streets that follow the shoreline, and you might get lost once or twice.

CORNWALL STORE
(1866)

The store on the waterfront, which now has local merchandise and historical exhibits, was established in the 1820s by Azariah Walton. He saw the potential for a steamboat stop before there was even a town. He had bought many of the islands in the area in order to cut the trees for steamboat fuel, and then sold the islands to people who would become his customers.

Pirates' Day celebration, Alexandria Bay.

Before the tourists arrived, the store and the wharf served mainly the farmers, the homes on the river, and the glassworks factory in Redwood. This gave Walton and his partners tremendous control of the local economy. Later, the grand Thousand Islands Hotel was built next door. Anything of any importance that happened in town, happened here. Like the area, the store suffered because of the stock market crash and closed at that time. The original store caught fire from the spark of a steamboat and was replaced with the current building. Some of the stone for the new building came from the penitentiary quarry in Kingston.

Walton was also one of the customs deputies. He and his partner tried to spur the growth of the town's commerce by giving the best spot on the waterfront to whoever would build a luxury hotel. As a result, the Thousand Islands House was built, in 1883, sixty years after Walton established his store. A hotel of this magnitude brought people to the river and awakened their interest in building on the islands. The hotel has since been demolished, but Azariah Walton knew what he was starting.

THE CHURCH OF ST. LAWRENCE
(1889)

Of all the churches in the islands, this one has one of the most interesting nautical histories. It was built like a lighthouse on a high rock promontory and its steeple is visible as a landmark to guide boaters on the river. The foundation is made of pink granite from the village quarry and the baptismal font is a massive piece of pink granite. The building was constructed by skiff builders from the village. They fitted together the small planks of oak and maple in the all-wood interior as though they were building a skiff. Parishioners say that the big arches inside the roof look like the beams of a boat. One of the stained-glass windows is dedicated to St. Lawrence and, in the background, is a scene of the Sunken Rock Lighthouse. The saint is standing over the pit of fire in which he was tortured.

An organist from the church, William Breitenbuecher, wrote the words and music for a hymn to St. Lawrence in 1988. One of the pastors says the hymn is almost like a country and western tune. A line from the hymn is as follows: "As our river flows from the lake into the sea, may the love of God flow through me."

SCENIC VIEW PARK

Across the street from the church is a great park for people who like to climb. It's a bit of a hike up and down, but there is a literally breathtaking view. You can see Boldt Castle from the park, as well as Sunken Rock Lighthouse, which was built in 1847. The lighthouse couldn't help every ship. In 1974, a large freighter struck the shoal upriver and sank down to the bottom.

ST. CYRIL'S
ROMAN CATHOLIC CHURCH
(1915–1922)

The architecture of many of the Catholic churches in the area ignored the island setting, but this one is different. St Cyril's was built like a castle, entirely of pink granite quarried from the site. It has a square tower and a red Mediterranean tile roof like Jorstadt Castle on the river. Because it is built on the side of a rock cliff, the front of the church is upstairs from the street. The back is level with Rock Street. Didn't Jesus say to build his church on a rock?

Construction began on the church in 1915, but was interrupted when the priest left for the First World War. Churches like this one are a reminder that the prestige of a community often lay in the magnificence of the church it could build. .

REFORMED CHURCH OF THE THOUSAND ISLES

(1848–1851)

This church was started by a minister from Philadelphia who came to the Thousand Islands for the fishing and was startled to find that the boy who rowed his boat didn't have a church where he could attend Sunday school. The minister put down his fishing rod and began preaching to people he found living in shacks on the islands or lounging in boats in the river. By the mid-1800s, he gathered enough support to build a permanent church and had time to start fishing again.

THE DEVIL'S OVEN

William Johnston had a hideout in the cave of a small island within sight of Alexandria Bay — or so the story goes. The island has a cave that's barely visible on the waterline and is almost inaccessible at times of high water. In fact, even when the conditions are right, it's almost inaccessible. The only entrance is by water. Apparently, Johnston's daughter Kate smuggled food to him in the islands when he was hiding. The cave is so small that it was given the name the Devil's Oven. Its actual size makes it unlikely that it could have been used for more than a temporary escape from the authorities.

Years after Johnston died, the Devil's Oven was cited in a sermon by the pastor of the Reformed Church of Alexandria Bay. The pastor was familiar with the story about Johnston's use of the Devil's Oven. He said the Devil's Oven was at the shoals of Hell's Gate. He used the renegade's refuge as an image of the part of the soul where people have "secret and rebellious thoughts" that tempt them from the righteous path.

✎ OTHER ATTRACTIONS ✎

Captain Graham Thomson Memorial Museum

AN IMMIGRANT'S KINGDOM
BOLDT CASTLE
(1900–1904)

All of us are driven to some degree by internal forces, but few of us like George Boldt. Boldt was obsessed by a compulsion to create a complete kingdom for himself in the Thousand Islands. At the age of thirteen, Boldt immigrated to the United States from the small Prussian island of Rugen, in the Baltic Sea. By the time he was fifty years old, he was the multi-millionaire operator of hotels including the Waldorf-Astoria in New York City. But he didn't stop there. In the late 1890s, when the Thousand Islands was becoming fashionable, he started buying property on islands and trans-forming them according to his master plan. The goal of his work, as the castle on Heart Island suggests, was to compensate for his earlier poverty by becoming the wealthy king and ruler of a small but elaborate kingdom. He built the one-hundred-and-twenty-room Boldt Castle, a giant yacht house that could berth a thirty-one-metre steam yacht with a tall mast, and a sys-tem of canals on Wellesley Island. The canals were designed to bring the produce of Boldt's island farm to his hotels by boat, although Boldt could have easily accomplished that without building the canals. Boldt's elaborate two-storey houseboat, with a stained-glass skylight, was aptly named for its part in his kingly design, *La Duchesse*. In all, he built five castlelike struc-tures on Heart Island. Ultimately Boldt, the kingdom builder, not only constructed his own duchy on an island, but the fame of his castle helped to popularize the Thousand Islands.

Boldt's kingdom came crashing to an end in 1904, when his wife Louise, the intended recipient of the castle, died suddenly of a heart attack at forty-one years of age. Boldt continued to come to the Thousand Islands, but he left the castle unfinished, and that seems be the symbolic end to the great flamboyant era of the islands. Over the years Boldt Castle has suc-cumbed to several indignities, such as a fire cause by fireworks and the stripping of its metal parts during the Second World War. As for Boldt, he died in a room at the Waldorf-Astoria at sixty-five years of age.

A store at Chippewa Bay.

CHIPPEWA BAY

HERMITS AND CASTLES

ROUTE 12 TO CHIPPEWA BAY

T HIS STRETCH OF THE RIVER is difficult to appreciate fully, unless you
have a boat and several years to wander. Even then it would be hard to do
it justice. This small part of the country specializes in social contrast, much
like a feudal kingdom. From the early 1800s, when the river was still a frontier, story after story accumulated about hermits, battles and hidden gold.
Then, in the late 1800s, the summer residents began to arrive, many of
them wealthy. This added yet another social layer.

OAK ISLAND

From Crooked Creek you can see Oak Island, which was used in just about
as many ways as an island can be. Today, it's mainly a nature preserve. The
island has caves that were first occupied by Indians and then adopted by the
children of the summer residents. At the turn of the century, Oak Island had
a quarry, which supplied the massive amounts of granite for the construction of Boldt Castle and Jorstadt Castle. After the quarries were finished,
the islanders took some of the earth to cover the bare-rock shoals. A man
named Dingman ran a farm here. Like other farmers on the islands, he
made good money in the 1920s selling milk, cream and vegetables to the
summer residents.

CHIPPEWA BAY & A BRIEF HISTORY OF ITS HERMITS

Chippewa Bay is named for the Indians of the area, who were called Chippewas or Ojibwas by the English and Saulteur or Mississauga by the French. Of course, everybody ignored the name they called themselves, which was the Anishinabeg.

Not many hermits in the world have a plaque commemorating them. But William McNeil, the first white settler of Chippewa Bay, does. McNeil came from Vermont sometime before 1812 and is thought to have been Irish. According to the plaque, "His home was a cave and he lived off the land." A hermit couldn't ask for a better epitaph, could he?

McNeil, as a hermit, set the tone for the early inhabitants. They came to the islands to get away from the disasters of humanity. Thus, in the western part of Chippewa Bay is Atlantis Island, where a runaway slave named Jack found sanctuary in the 1840s. The location was so remote at that time that he didn't have to cross into Canada to feel distant from the United States. On an island next door to Jack's island there lived another runaway slave named Joe.

The hermits and runaway slaves found plenty to eat. The islands in the area were full of wild raspberries and huckleberries and the river had plenty of fish. There was also game to hunt. The early islanders must have had food on their minds, because many places were named for something edible. Islands were named for choke cherries, bilberries, corn, and grapes. Points of land tended to be named after the fish that could be caught there. And small islands commemorated the birds that could be shot and eaten. Many of the other names came from British navy surveyors in the early 1800s, who usually named islands after obscure British navy officers and warships.

In the 1840s, Chippewa Bay had a character named Ezra Brockway. He was known to some as an old Civil War veteran but to others as just a hermit. He lived on an island, mixed batches of a magical salve from pitch pine, and told people a wild tale about being the son of Napoleon Bonaparte. Many men in the Cape Vincent area, which began as a French settlement with ties to the Corsican, were given the name Napoleon but never claimed to be his children.

As the legend of the hermit grew in the years after his death, people began to dig on the island for the gold they assumed he had buried there. For some reason, people think hermits are wealthy. In this case, there were other rumours that added to the stories of treasure on the island. It was believed that gold stolen from a British supply boat was either buried on the hermit's island or sunk in the water nearby. The most plausible story was that a group of pirates known as the Patterson gang intercepted a boat carrying gold. The money was meant to pay the British troops at Kingston around the time of the War of 1812. The pirates took the gold and their captives up Chippewa Creek. The British caught the gang on an island and killed Patterson, who died with the secret of where the gold was hidden. Naturally this amount of hidden gold kept the local people busy hunting for years. And so it happened in 1906 that Chippewa Bay was thrown into an uproar when a gang of outsiders came searching at night for gold that the river people naturally considered their own.

Chippewa Bay was once a thriving community. Granite, timber and iron ore were shipped out of the bay in tremendous quantities. It was here that Captain James Denner operated a fleet of two-masted schooners. Some of the timber and ore was taken to islands at the edge of the bay to be picked up by ships. Chippewa Bay had a hotel, a glass factory, a cheese factory, a shipyard, a schoolhouse, a racetrack, and blacksmith shops. In April of 1865, a steamboat brought news that President Lincoln had been assassinated. Later, a small troop of cavalry came through the village looking for the assassin. The fortunes of Chippewa Bay sank with the end of the timber and the arrival of the railroads. As for Captain Denner, he went down with one of his ships in Lake Ontario.

At the outer extremity of the bay, close to the main shipping channel of the seaway, is the Cedar Island cluster of islands, which has been a little summer colony since the late 1800s. It was the choice of the artist Frederic Remington, a bit of a hermit himself. By the 1890s, Cedar Island had a hotel, general store and post office, where steamboats could stop on their way from Ogdensburg to Clayton. In those days the summer residents carried a lot of luggage by steamer, even a piano if they wanted it.

REMINGTON'S ISLAND

By the time Frederic Remington had become famous as an illustrator of the Wild West, he had purchased an island in Chippewa Bay, and came here every summer from 1900 to 1908. This was the most creative — and final — period of his life. His diary shows that he delighted in the everyday details of life — windstorms on the river, the lightning that struck his apple tree, a night so quiet that he wrote, "I heard a dog in Canada bark." He enjoyed the isolation and open space of the river, and so could joke about Chippewa Bay as "the only place in N[orth] America which is as still as death." Remington liked to bluster on his island and wanted to feel that he was on the frontier again exposed to the elements. One entry in his diary — "it thunderstormed most awfully" — sounds as though he imagined himself to be like Huckleberry Finn on his raft. Remington, as a painter, built his studio on the north point of the island to get the best light; a river person would have chosen the south side to get the warmth of the sun. On his island Remington could paint undisturbed, fish for bass if he wanted, or observe the herons and the muskrats.

Remington adored the spot and came here so early some years that it was too cold to paint. He said at one point, "I want to get out on those rocks by my studio in the early morning while the birds are singing and the sun ashining and hop in among the bass. When I die my heaven is going to be something like that." The neighbourhood was spoiled, to some extent, for Remington by the construction of Jorstadt Castle across the water from

Trilliums under the Thousand Islands bridge.

his island. Remington would sit on his porch and scowl at the pretentious castle as it was being built.

Mainly for his own artistic satisfaction, Remington would float across the water and make sketches under the big August moon. It was on the island that he perfected his own way to paint moonlight. He also dressed the river people in costumes and had them paddle in front of his cottage so that he could draw apparently authentic scenes of Indians on the river. One of his models for an Indian was the man who ran the hotel on Cedar Island. Remington also asked the islanders to sit on a stuffed bucking bronco in his studio so that he could have models of cowboys. He abhorred the toads on his island and paid boys a nickel apiece to get rid of them. The boys made the supply of toads last longer by importing them from other islands. Before he had been there ten years, Remington sold the island. The local people wanted to believe he left because of losses on the stock market, but, in fact, he needed the money for other reasons. He died the same year.

BIG WINDS IN THE BAY

Chippewa Bay, if it was good enough for deserters, runaway slaves and hermits, was good enough for rum-runners too. Like everybody else who lived here, they appreciated its remoteness. They brought in booze and illegal immigrants and kept the summer residents content with liquor. One spot where they landed was Blind Bay, just behind Chippewa Point. As the name suggests, it was a perfect spot because it was hidden and the road was nearby.

Otherwise, the islands in the bay were the summer home for people from the cities who found a permanence to life here that they couldn't find elsewhere. As one of the summer people remarked, "It may look to others like a snake-infested pile of rocks, but to me it is my ancestral home."[6] The summer residents were especially vulnerable to summer romances. Many fell in love quickly and married under the spell of the river. Often they returned to the river yearly to keep the romance going, which started the

*P*ainting the domes of the Kingston city hall.

Sunken Rock Lighthouse seen through the rain from the deck of a freighter.

Devil's Oven, the island near Alexandria Bay where renegade William Johnston hid in a cave (barely visible at the waterline).

The figurehead of a wooden ship docked in Kingston.

More charming than the regal Boldt Castle, Jorstadt Castle sits in an isolated part of the river between Chippewa Bay and Mallorytown Landing.

TOP: *Boldt Castle, near Alexandria Bay, epitomizes the grandeur of the golden era of the Thousand Islands, from the late 1800s to the early 1900s.* BOTTOM: *Once every summer, battles between the British and the Americans are recreated at Fort Wellington, Prescott.*

For years Cape Vincent grocery store owner Charles Aubrey played the role of Napoleon in the town's French Festival.

TOP: *The entrance of the Densmore church, Wellesley Island, is through a round turret.*
BOTTOM: *The international bridge, between Johnstown and Ogdensburg, is visible from the harbour at Prescott.*

TOP: *An airboat crosses the ice off an island near Clayton.* BOTTOM: *The Wolfe Island ferry dock with the domes of St. George's Cathedral in the background.*

For boys in Ogdensburg, one of the best fishing holes is a pond by an abandoned factory.

River painter Michael Ringer sketches a lily pad from his boat.

One of the last independent commercial fishermen in the area works near Gananoque.

Hunters return from a swamp near Alexandria Bay.

In the summertime, boys from Cape Vincent jump from the back of the Horne ferry.

Giving the Canadian span of the Thousand Islands Bridge, near Ivy Lea, a coat of forest-green paint.

A great blue heron basks in the warmth of the setting sun.

cycle all over again with their children. The oldest ones remember collecting water lilies in Crooked Creek, going berry picking on the islands, and swatting bats at night with tennis rackets. They even recall the big wind in the 1930s that blew the floor of Addison Strong's house off his island and down the river with his shotgun propped against his rocking chair.

In 1955, the summer residents bought the store in Chippewa Bay and started to operate it as a collective so that no one could gouge them over the prices. It was called the Chippewa Bay Company.

CROSSOVER ISLAND LIGHTHOUSE
(1848)

Crossover Island got its name as the point in the river where ships could take either the American channel to the south or the Canadian channel to the north. Because it was such an exposed place in the river, the lighthouse keeper had to rescue hundreds of sailors.

MORRISTOWN

It's worth driving around the streets of Morristown just to get a sense of the optimism of the original settlers who built houses on such rough, rocky, unruly ground. The view is great and the old stone windmill built on the highest point of land gives one a sense of exhilaration. The streets here are so steep that you'd think people would roll down them into the river.

Morristown, built precariously on a rock cliff, was exposed to trade wars between the British and the Americans and battles along the river before it contracted to its present size. It was from here, during the War of 1812, that Major Benjamin Forsyth launched his raid on Brockville across the ice. Look across the river and you'll see just how close Brockville is. Forsyth hired a tavern keeper from the village to help take the troops across the frozen river to Brockville, where they surprised the soldiers in their beds. It just wasn't safe on the border when the river froze.

In the last half of the 1800s, this was a thriving industrial town. The major industry was the manufacture of Dr. Morse's Indian Root Pills, which were a mixture of just about every imaginable ingredient intended to cure just about every imaginable illness. The company was owned by a Brockville family named Comstock that came originally from New York City. The pill factory, with about fifty workers at its peak, got a boost when the railway came to the river in 1876. Most of the pills were sent abroad — to the west, the Orient and South America. Of course, there was no Dr. Morse. He was a fictional creation to make the medicine more salable. The company also produced such toothsome products as Judson's Worm Tea. The factory brought the village into the twentieth century, by which time its population had swelled to seven hundred. It operated until 1960. The factory building is now used as a marina.

THE STONE WINDMILL
(1825)

After all the hard work that went into building a stone mill in the 1820s, the owner didn't get much use out if it. The business had milled grain for only a year when the owner drowned and the operation ceased. The windmill was converted into a jail with circular cells in the 1880s. During the Second World War it became a lookout post for German warplanes. The view was great but the planes never came.

A restaurant in Morristown.

This lighthouse in Ogdensburg has been converted into a home.

OGDENSBURG

AN OSWEGATCHIE SUMMER

ABBÉ FRANCOIS PICQUET, of the Sulpician order, had no fear of the wilderness. An adventurous man, he crossed the ocean from France and, in 1749, arrived at the mouth of the Oswegatchie River to start a mission for the Indians. The priest chose the perfect location for a mission. Anybody travelling on the river was obliged to pass this spot because of the narrow channel. There was also a sheltered bay here in a part of the river that, even in the winters of the 1700s, was slow to freeze.

Picquet and priests like him were worth their weight in gold to the army. Unlike the soldiers, they had taken the time to learn the languages of the Iroquois and the Algonquin, and so they could talk to them. The priests weren't afraid of a little bloodshed either, and worked at the scenes of battles as spiritual advisors. Picquet in particular made it to the hot spots of his time. During the Seven Years' War he went, with troops from Fort Frontenac, to the battle near Fort Ticonderoga and he was present at several other battles as well.

In those days there was little separation between the church and the military. The fort La Presentation was built with the chapel inside one of the fortified corners and one of the priests even drilled the Indians in French military exercises. Picquet fell into power struggles with one of the military commanders of the fort. One time he even left the mission for a while because he felt that the military commander was asserting too much authority.

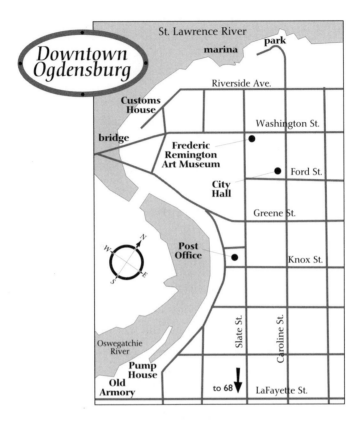

Picquet had some success with his mission and fortified post. Two years after he established it there were four hundred Indians here. But, with the defeat of the French a little more than a decade later, he was soon gone. Fort Frontenac (at what would later become Kingston) fell to the British in 1758. Two years later the French made their last stand in the river near Picquet's mission. There was a bloody battle between ships, and, typical for the times, a French ship was captured, refitted for use by the British, and then sunk by the French.

The French retreated to Fort de Levis, an island that had been hastily fortified with walls along the shoreline. It was meant to replace Fort Frontenac after that fort's fall to the British, and would have been an ideal fortress to control the river if it had been constructed properly. After retreating to the island, the French suffered a bombardment and fires for two days before they surrendered. Meanwhile Picquet, as though he were a pirate, had a price on his head. He was forced to flee Canada. His fort was destroyed by the French and the Indians as they left. The cornerstone of Picquet's fort was later fixed in the wall of the new town hall at Ogdensburg after being rescued from a fire in the old town hall.

BUILDING A COMMUNITY

In the years leading up to the War of 1812, Ogdensburg became a commercial rival of Kingston and Prescott, but without the military ambitions of those two places. The community was developed by a land speculator named Samuel Ogden. He laid out the plans, along with his land agent, but never came here himself. The Americans arrived to settle in 1796. It seemed like a good place to establish a port and shipbuilding centre that could compete with Kingston and perhaps break the hold of the merchants there. But that ambition was frustrated by the U.S. Embargo Act of 1807, which banned the import of British goods. The ban may have seemed reasonable for those who had to cross the ocean to get British goods. But, along the St. Lawrence River, it was only a short distance to trade for British materials. Here, the embargo seemed like a way of punishing your own people to hurt the enemy. The embargo more or less forced the Ogdensburg merchants to be smugglers if they wanted to be successful. Trade was further threatened with the outbreak of war in 1812, leaving Ogdensburg in an ambivalent position. The people of Ogdensburg would have preferred not to have a war. Their settlement wasn't fortified at the time of the War of 1812, so it might have quietly passed through the war if not for an American troublemaker named

Major Benjamin Forsyth and an equally troublesome British commander named Red George Macdonell.

During the War of 1812, the British crossed the ice on the river to capture a few U.S. troops at Ogdensburg. It was more of an insult than an attack, but the Yankees, under the agitator Forsyth, were creating all sorts of bad feelings along the border by raids. Forsyth retaliated against the meagre attack on Ogdensburg with a larger force that freed the prisoners in Brockville and took British prisoners and supplies. At that point the British had a dilemma: they wanted to defend their country, but they didn't want to retaliate and create a military hot zone. They decided not to retaliate. However, when Red George, a Scotsman with red hair and a fiery temper, was left in command at Prescott across the river, he ignored his orders and answered the Brockville incident with a still larger force that invaded Ogdensburg. Red George's men crossed the ice dragging cannons with them and took prisoners again.

After that, nobody wanted to fight over Ogdensburg. The local people didn't want to be a military target or to see the river community divided by the war. After the citizens of Ogdensburg cheered the withdrawal of American soldiers, they petitioned the governor to prevent the return of their own troops. The settlement became a kind of unprotected free zone during the war and a place that British officers could visit for dinner. The Americans also went to dine in Fort Wellington at Prescott. One American merchant traded from Ogdensburg during the war using the King's ships. The Americans sold beef to the army across the river, which concerned the British, who thought that this kind of smuggling would help the enemy to spy on them.

In 1850, the railway arrived in Ogdensburg, which led to a reorganization of the waterfront and initially increased shipping. A ferry service was started to carry railway cars back and forth between Ogdensburg and Prescott, which lasted more than eighty years. The ferry survived longer than some of the other ferries on the St. Lawrence because a bridge wasn't opened across this section of the river until 1960. Eventually, as with Kingston, the ships lost the battle to the railways, which lost it again to highways, and the waterfront was transformed accordingly. When the influence of shipping deteriorated, parts of Ogdensburg decayed, leaving derelict buildings as monuments to the economic change.

These days Ogdensburg has a wide stretch of park land along the waterfront that's good for watching the river and the ships at any time except during shadfly season. The shadflies fill the air in plague-like proportions. However, the insect is a perfectly harmless nuisance and is taken by some people as a sign of a healthy river.

The Greater Ogdensburg Chamber of Commerce has organized a walking tour of battlefield sites from the War of 1812 and other wars in the waterfront area. The chamber issues a brochure so that visitors can guide themselves to the points of interest.

THE FREDERIC REMINGTON ART MUSEUM

Frederic Sackrider Remington, the man who helped to create the popular image of the American West through his illustrations and paintings, was born nearby in Canton and lived in Ogdensburg as a boy. His father, a cavalry major in the Civil War, led a charge of eighty-six men against Confederate forces of 1,800. He returned exhilarated but with sixty-eight fewer men. His son, the artist, continued the military tradition by painting scenes of the Old West and of men at war.

Not so well known are the scenes that Remington painted of rivers. He spent the last decade of his life painting in the summers on an island near Chippewa Bay. The work that he did on the river allowed him to experiment with colour and scenery and a frontier different from the Old West. A painting of his called *Breaking up the Ice in the Spring* reveals something most river people already know — the ice in the Thousand Islands is

A work barge passes the Thousand Islands International Bridge.

green during break-up. A poster that was made of this painting mistakenly adjusted the colour of the ice to blue. Remington died in 1909 and was buried under a simple gravestone in the Evergreen Cemetery in Canton. The Remington Museum in Ogdensburg has the largest collection of the artist's work on the continent.

HARBOUR LIGHTHOUSE
(1900)

The piece of land, known today as Lighthouse Point, and visible from the waterfront, has been through a long cycle of use. It started as the mission and Indian settlement of Abbé Picquet. The priest built his mission here, at the mouth of the Oswegatchie River, and organized a colony of Indians, called the Oswegatchie Indians. In essence, Picquet created a new tribe by bringing together Indians from different tribes. After the fort was abandoned, the peninsula was used as the quarantine point for the cholera epidemic of 1832. Later it was used as the shipyard, a railway depot and a lighthouse station. Finally the peninsula became a nice place to live, as Abbé Picquet had originally intended.

A Coast Guard ship at Prescott.

PRESCOTT

IT "BOILED AND BUBBLED STRANGELY"

T
HE PART OF THE RIVER that Victorians like Charles Dickens enjoyed the most was the rapids. In 1842, Dickens travelled through the area. His description of Kingston was dull and laboured. He struggled for the words to describe the islands. But when he passed Prescott and rode the rapids in a steamboat, he loved the bumpy ride. It made him feel like a kid again. The river, he wrote in his travelogue, was "strange" the way it "bubbled" and "boiled." The force was "tremendous," he said. Others took pleasure in finding inventive ways to describe the rapids. It was fun for them to be jostled and shaken and splashed in a steamboat full of people. They loved to feel the power of the river. Thomas Hamilton from Philadelphia said that the Long Sault rapids had "a thundering roar." Another traveller, Robert Baird from Great Britain, talked about the excitement of shooting the rapids "with the speed of a sea bird." Luckily for them they didn't suffer the discomforts that the poorer travellers did — the crowded decks, the fierce storms, and the cold water. In the days before steamboats men had died in the rapids. The rapids were so bad that the British and French lost more soldiers in the water than were killed in the bloody siege of the French fort on an island nearby.

Prescott was bustling with business by the time Dickens passed it on a steamboat. The land had been settled in the late 1700s on a large grant

109

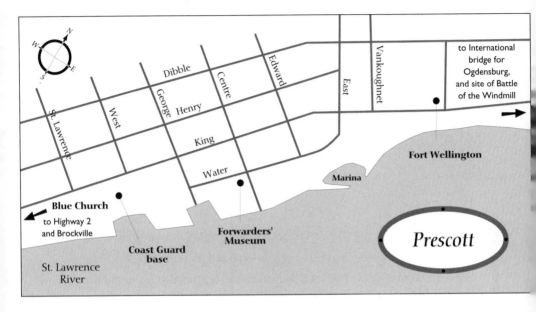

belonging to Colonel Edward Jessup, who commanded a group of Loyalists during the American Revolution. One of Jessup's strong points during the war was his enthusiasm for recruiting soldiers, which some people believed went too far. He enlisted captured rebels, German mercenaries, and even children too young to join legally, such as a twelve-year-old orphan. In the end, Jessup was on the losing side of the war along with the other Loyalists. By coming to Prescott he could look across the river and think how his life had changed with the revolution.

Jessup and others realized the importance of Prescott's location on the river. Prescott was upriver from the rapids and thus a natural place to stop to load and unload boats. It grew like a frontier town in the Old West, with cargo piling up, and crowds of people landing by boat and staying a day or two. The crowds got so large that hundreds of passengers had to wait in tents before resuming their voyage. Some people found Prescott "a miserable village." The place was filled with throngs of sailors, passengers and soldiers, all looking for diversions.

With its prosperity tied to the rapids, all went well in Prescott until the mid-1800s. Until that time, nothing could compete with the skill of the men who took the boats through the rapids. Even elaborate schemes, such as moving cargo around the rapids by covered wagons mounted on rails, never amounted to anything. But canals were opened in the 1840s, followed by the railroad in 1854. That changed the pattern of transportation. Then, a century later, the St. Lawrence Seaway opened in 1959. With the seaway, the river was flooded and the bite taken out of the rapids. The boats no longer had to stop at Prescott. Transportation by road was also taking business from the boats. One of the men responsible for this change in transportation along the river was Henry Ford. He didn't come by car, though. He docked here in 1919 to show off his new yacht.

Prescott never became a shipbuilding centre, and yet it was an important port. Fourteen steamboats a week departed from here at the time of Dickens's visit, and the large luxury passenger ship the *Great Britain* was built here and launched in 1830. In the newspapers of the day, the ship was called the "Leviathan of the lake," "Monarch of the Marine," and "floating palace." One account has it that the ship was built with more imagination than went into writing *The Arabian Nights*. It could hold one thousand travellers and its decks were often packed with immigrants. As luck would have it, the *Great Britain*, with its four grand smoke stacks, invited the kind of misadventures that were typical on the river. The ship was struck by lightning, a man committed suicide by jumping off it, and a British deserter was seized on board and then freed by Americans. Once, at night, the ship also struck and sank a schooner. In spite of the luxury of the steamboat, a decade after it was built, plans were being made to dismantle it. One suggestion was that the steamboat be used in Kingston as a floating hotel for the parliament of the country.

The rum trade was well supported by the grog shops of Prescott, and distilleries were built on the water. The port was convenient for shipping the liquor out. The distillery here was so big that it employed sixty workers and required three government officials to collect the duties. The mash from the distillery was used to fatten herds of cattle, and so the operation made many people happy.

COAST GUARD STATION

One of the town's remaining ties to the river is the Canadian Coast Guard Station. The location was originally picked in 1903 for the Dominion Lighthouse Depot, which was responsible for manufacturing lights for the country's lighthouses. Later it was converted for the Coast Guard. The station is the base for two icebreakers and is responsible for the safety of navigation between the Beauharnois Canal, near Montreal, and Grand Bend, on Lake Huron.

FORWARDERS' MUSEUM

The rapids upriver from Prescott required some courage to navigate. Out of this difficulty grew a group called forwarders who moved the cargo through the rapids and along the river. The forwarding trade began here in 1810 even before the first wooden blockhouse was constructed. The freight boats, carrying either cargo or passengers, were gathered in groups to help with portages. Sometimes the boats were pulled with ropes by oxen or horses. After the rapids the cargo was loaded into a fleet of sailing schooners and steamboats. Business was good for the forwarders. They could charge whatever fee they wanted and so they naturally banded together to set prices.

One forwarder was the fiery, domineering Irishman, Timothy Buckley. Buckley came from County Cork in Ireland to Canada after his wife died. Encouraged by the opportunity that he saw, he went back to Ireland for his daughter, and returned to Canada with a new wife. While his wife was bearing and raising seven children, Buckley established himself as one of the leading forwarders in Prescott.

WATER STREET

Many sailors, soldiers and immigrants passed through Prescott, and the town was able to support a street of taverns with names like the Pigeon Hole, the Black Bull, the Dolphin, and the Dog and Duck. At that time, Water Street was a noisy frontier road with drunken men, fiddlers and prostitutes, although, with the number of soldiers on hand, it was probably not as lawless as streets in the American West. The shops that catered to ships were also located here, and it was an ideal spot to lounge, smoke a clay pipe and watch the world go by.

European immigrants brought with them the epidemics that were widespread at the time in Europe. During the cholera epidemic, the immigrants who were infected in the Prescott area were isolated on an island in the river. People who had come across the ocean to escape the old country and its problems died here from a disease they brought with them.

Prescott was linked to Ogdensburg, on the American side of the river, since the early 1800s. At that time, a ferry ran across the river, and when the river froze in the wintertime it was easy to move across the ice. The frozen river also made it convenient to cross the border and either steal or smuggle cattle. According to some stories, the hotels and buildings in Prescott had large underground tunnels leading to the river that were used for smuggling tea, cotton and guns across the water. During the years of political turmoil the border was also useful. If anything was going wrong on one side of the border, the other side provided sanctuary.

FORT WELLINGTON

(1838–1839)

The British were perpetually lagging at Prescott. They started a fort in 1813, with the War of 1812 already underway. The fort was built slowly and wasn't finished until the peace treaty was signed. It never saw an attack during the war, although it did get a chance to fire its guns. That was on a night in 1813, when the invasion fleet of Major General John Wilkinson was passing on the river. Thousands of men were on their way down the river to the Battle of Crysler's Farm, devouring farms along the way like hungry wolves. The British took this opportunity to fire their cannons at them, although this was more a display of fireworks over the river than a strategic attack. After the War of 1812, the fort was left to fall in ruins. Then an American invasion during the Rebellion of 1837 — known as the Battle of the Windmill — gave the British the incentive to finish the fort.

A few years ago at Fort Wellington, archaeologists dug up the site of the latrine, which has the distinction of being the oldest military privy in Canada. They were able to analyze it for clues about everyday life at the fort. The latrine was built in 1838 with a pit made out of durable stone. It was used as a garbage dump and so the archaeologists found fancy broken crockery, clay pipes, women's combs, women's boots, and fish and cow bones. There were also signs — such as porcelain marbles and turn-of-the-century German porcelain dolls with glass eyes — that children were billeted in the barracks with their families.

It was considered a privilege for families of the soldiers to be allowed to live in the barracks. Six soldiers out of every company of one hundred were allowed to have their families with them. A bed would be curtained off for the couple and it was customary at the time for children to either sleep under the bed or to take a cot left empty by a sentry on duty. The soldiers at the fort were also allowed the added incentive of making money by moonlighting outside the fort. Some of them had homes in the town. The

British relaxed the rules about families living in the barracks at Fort Wellington to try and stop the high number of desertions to the United States.

❧ OTHER SIGHTS ❧

Church of St. Mark the Evangelist (1888)

THE BATTLE OF THE WINDMILL

The old windmill, built out of limestone from the area in 1822, has seen a lot of history on the river, particularly since it was the site of the bloodiest battle of the region in the mid-1800s.

It all started in 1837, the year that Queen Victoria came to the throne. A rebellion erupted in Upper Canada led by a small, intense man named William Lyon Mackenzie. Rebels like Mackenzie didn't like to be governed by people who weren't elected. Eventually Mackenzie would discover that he didn't like the democratic system of the United States any better and he would be thrown in prison there. But that was after the rebellion fizzled in Upper Canada.

The biggest battle of the rebellion took place in the Prescott area, with Mackenzie elsewhere and the disturbance moving at its own pace. The Americans, who looked a lot like pirates and invaders to Canadians, swarmed across the river in boats, full of grand delusions about the people who lived north of the border. The Americans were great advocates of rebellion; the date of their own had been declared a national holiday. At the time of the rebellion in Canada, they formed secret societies called Hunters Lodges and planned attacks to coincide with Washington's birthday and Independence Day. They intended to awaken the citizens in Canada to independence, however, it never occurred to them that Canadians didn't celebrate Washington's birthday. The Canadians were as unrevolutionary as you could get. They had a different idea of patriotism and saw themselves as defenders of the independence they already had from Americans. The Americans came across the river as an international Republican brigade; they were in for a surprise.

The outcome of the attack would depend on how both sides used the ships available to them. The British, warned in advance, had prepared for the fight by bringing ships into the area. The rebels, who initially crossed the river with two schooners loaded with men and boys, didn't provide boats in case of retreat — a typical flaw of American enthusiasm. The rebels' lack of skill in navy manoeuvres was clear after what happened. The schooner commanded by William Johnston got stuck in the soft mud in the delta of the Oswegatchie River at Ogdensburg.

The Canadians fought their liberators and forced them back into an abandoned stone windmill that became a makeshift fort. It was here that things started to look bleak for the Americans, including their unfortunate commander, Count Nils von Schoultz. The two sides fought for a while, took a break to bury their dead, then started fighting again. People in Ogdensburg had a good vantage point and watched, from across the river. The battle, in the light of the burning houses, stood out against the dark clouds of the day. The people in Prescott, who were closer to the battle, didn't have the same luxury. One woman, who was a girl at the time, remembers hiding inside a grandfather clock during the battle. A cannon shot from a British steamboat beheaded a young man named Solomon Foster, who was the pilot at the wheel of an American steamboat seized by the American invaders.

Eventually, with the Americans cut off from help by armed British steamboats on the river, the windmill was captured. At the end of the battle, twenty dead bodies were scattered around the windmill, and about one hundred and fifty prisoners had to be transported to Fort Henry at Kingston, the biggest available jail. The aftermath was hard for the families involved, with the prisoners either being hanged or exiled. The dislocation after the battle may have caused more lasting harm than the battle itself. Among the prisoners were boys of fourteen and fifteen years, who had been swept along by the excitement of the liberation. There were heart-breaking stories, such as that of Orrin Blodgett, who took the place of his teenage brother to have him released from his enlistment in the invading army. For his trouble, Blodgett was transported to Van Diemen's Land, now Tasmania, with about sixty others. Thirteen years later, after many adventures, he returned home.

After the battle, some of the local people, out of irritation, fired at a few American ships on the river. A mob in Prescott stole a cannon from an American ship to replace one stolen by the invaders. The windmill, which had begun its life grinding grist and then saw so much bloodshed, was turned into a lighthouse in 1873.

BLUE CHURCH (1845)

As the Bible says, "some seeds fall on hard ground and other seeds find good soil and nourishment." So it was here. The first church at this location was built in the early 1800s for a community that was conceived by the Loyalist soldier Justus Sherwood but never developed. Others, too, had the dream of building a community here. One was as an Anglican priest from England, the Reverend Robert Blakey. The stone rectory he built opposite the grave-yard now stands as a monument to a ghost town. Reverend Blakey is buried here with a tombstone shaped like a small church with a peaked roof.

Also buried here are Barbara Heck and her husband. They fled the United States at the time of the American Revolution, after building the first church for Methodism in North America. They earned a footnote in history for helping to change the nature of religion on the continent. Barbara Heck died while reading a Bible and was buried in the graveyard before there was even a church. Meanwhile, Methodism spread quickly in

117

The Blue Church.

the farm communities on the mainland and the islands. Methodists also set up large summer camps along the river.

MAITLAND

It seems as if the current of the river slows here and, with it, the troubles and pace of life. Even the old trees in this place look like they have a history. Maitland is unusual as a largely intact stone village from the 1830s. It was never absorbed into a larger community as time went on, so it's a good place to catch a glimpse of the past. Even at the time the buildings were constructed, they were probably intended to awaken a sense of nostalgia for the old country.

In the mid-1800s, Maitland was a lively community with a blacksmith, four inns and a small port operation. One of the landmarks from that time is the grey shell of a windmill built on the waterfront in 1828 to grind the grain brought by boat. Later, the structure became a distillery for rye whisky, which was easy to dispense from its location right on the river. As the river flowed, so did the whisky. The distillery supported the industry of barrel making here until the owners of the rye operation were closed down for failing to pay the taxes.

Of course, the combination of liquor and the river at Maitland led to smuggling. At one time, a customs agent was sent here to strike terror into the hearts of the smugglers. The smugglers, in turn, threatened to blow his brains out. That was the kind of adventure that went with life on the border.

Across the street from the windmill is the Dumbrille home. The building, with a low stone wall, looks sober on the outside, but inside it has a quiet sense of dignity and elegance. The home, built in 1837, got its name from the prominent Dumbrille who bought it twenty years later. Dumbrille was a merchant, druggist, postmaster, railway agent, justice of the peace and finally, reeve of the township. In any other time and place the concentration of so much power and money might have alarmed people.

This Dumbrille apparently never did. When people fell into debt with him, he let them work their way out instead of squeezing them for money.

ST. JAMES ANGLICAN CHURCH
(1826)

Talk about humility in architecture. This church foregoes the grand entrance of large doors common to many churches. Instead, it has two separate single doors that lead directly to the two aisles of the church. The bell of the church was consecrated in 1873. It was a bequest that was meant to recall the memory of an entire family when it roused the villagers. The church still has some of the old box pews. One of the pastors was buried near the church in a stone vault because he was afraid his grave would be robbed by medical students.

POINTE–AU–BARIL

After the fall of Fort Frontenac in 1758, the French needed a new shipyard to build ships to protect the river and the Great Lakes. They found the location here at what became the site of one of the earliest French forts and shipyards on the upper St. Lawrence River. The result was the kind of combination that's appropriate for the river — a fortified shipyard. The French built a log fort here in 1758. Nearby they built two warships. One of the ships was damaged by rocks in the river. The other took a lone stand against the invasion fleet of Amherst at the time of the Seven Years' War. After a bloody fight between vessels, the French ship was forced to surrender to the British. The French ship was then used by the British to attack the nearby French outpost, Fort de Levis. In the late 1700s, a school was opened in a building inside the old fort.

The dam on the Gananoque River inside the town of Gananoque.

Brockville cityscape with the spires of the Wall Street United Church.

BROCKVILLE

O NE OF THE MOST important tourists and travel writers of the late 1800s, Mark Twain, stopped in Brockville on a stormy winter night in 1885. He was travelling along the river by rail, not by steamboat, as his precursor, Charles Dickens, had done forty years before him. Twain, distracted by larger issues, thought he was in a place called Brockton. But those things happen to travellers. Twain was in Canada to protect the copyright of his latest book, *Huckleberry Finn*, against Canadian pirates who might publish the book on their own for profit.

It was a blustery time for everyone when Twain arrived in Brockville. The newspaper was full of stories about the fall of Khartoum and speculated about the death of the British officer Major-General Charles Gordon. The ice was thick on the river and the steamboat ferry from Ogdensburg — which operated "wind and weather permitting" — was struggling to cut a channel for itself. The customs agents were busy trying to catch boys who were smuggling cans of coal oil across the ice from Morristown. That evening, with the snowstorm still raging, the Grand Opera House was filled with people who paid twenty-five cents to hear the famous writer. They said that just looking at him made them laugh. Twain read a passage from *Huckleberry Finn*. Then he retired for the night and slept in the best inn in town. The local newspaper thought it was

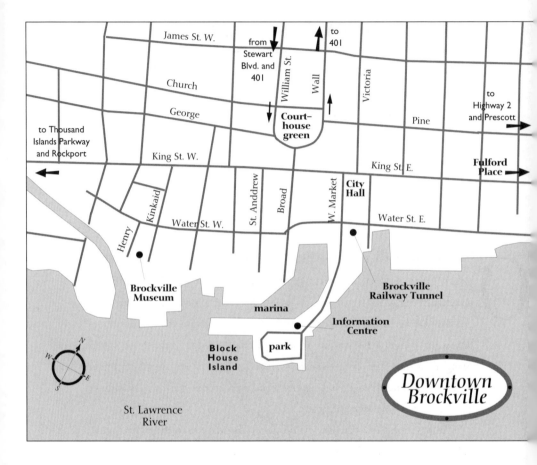

Downtown Brockville

worth mentioning that a sixty-year-old groom was celebrating his marriage in the same hotel that night.

At that time, Brockville was a settlement of ten thousand souls. The town was laid out by William Buell, a Loyalist soldier who liked the look of Connecticut towns.

In 1785, Buell took a long sloping section of land near the water that was unfit for farming. Over the years, he increased the land's value and his own prominence by virtually giving pieces of land away to build a courthouse and churches. Buell laid out the plan for the regal boulevard running from a hill down towards the river. Because of the terraced effect of the slope here, and throughout the settlement, many of the buildings still offer a view of the river. Another result of Buell's foresight was the square in the centre of the Brockville, called Courthouse Green. It's unusual in the area for the elegance and grandeur of the setting. Originally Courthouse Green had four large churches and the building that is the county courthouse today. A fire destroyed one of the churches. Three of the churches from the late 1800s — the First Baptist Church (1879), the First Presbyterian Church (1878) and the Wall Street Methodist Church (1830), now a United Church — remain standing.

High up on the courthouse roof is the figure of a woman holding the scales of justice. The figure is a replica of the original statue made when the current courthouse was built in the 1840s. The original figure was carved of white cedar. The artist was William Holmes, a man from England who once carved the figureheads on ships.[7] According to one story, the statue was named Sally Grant as a joke. The joke was that the towering statue must be the offspring of Major Alexander Grant, a very tall man who was in the crowd when the figure was raised. Sally Grant suffered many indignities over a century. She stood through rain and snow, was painted a garish red, and was retired to a garage in the 1950s. Her replica was erected in 1982. The original was rescued for a museum in the village of Westport, north of here.

Fifty years after Buell settled here, his family played an important role in arousing the sentiments for political reform that helped to inspire the Rebellion of 1837. The leader of the rebellion, William Lyon Mackenzie, stayed in the Buell home and the family ran a Reform newspaper in Brockville. But this was a Canadian version of rebellion, which led a cautious reformer like William Buell Jr. to write in his newspaper: "Yet we would rather suffer the evils under which we labour, than plunge the country into others we know not of."

Not everyone was convinced of the need for caution, though, and during the rebellion, one of Brockville's citizens, Donald McLeod, a teacher, acted as a general in the American force. He later worked for the Canadian government. Another citizen, John Berry, was taken prisoner during the Battle of the Windmill. He too was sentenced to the penal colony in Van Diemen's Land and, returned home twenty years later.

Brockville was never a significant British military post, even though it was renamed after the daring British commander General Isaac Brock. Brockville got its name in 1812, the year that Brock died in battle near Niagara. Over the years, the town largely escaped the tensions along the border. One exception was the raid led by the American commander Major Benjamin Forsyth during the War of 1812. During that raid, in 1813, prisoners were released from the jail. The Americans attacked by walking across the ice.

THE WATERFRONT

Brockville's location on the river has always been one of its strengths. Ships made regular stops here, and the community was once linked to Morristown, on the other side of the river, by ferry. By the 1830s, Brockville had shipbuilding yards where steamboats, schooners and barges were constructed. In those days the launching of a ship was a social occasion, with the church bells ringing and guns firing salutes. The steamboat *Sir Robert Peel* was built here in 1837 and burned the next year by rebels. The shipbuilding industry wasn't as strong in Brockville as it was in Kingston and Clayton. It virtually closed down in the 1860s.

By the early 1900s, Brockville had a district of mansions built by wealthy people along the waterfront bluff on its east side. Many of the original mansions still stand today. One of the most visible signs of wealth in the community was the elegant, forty-metre steam yacht of the politician George Fulford. His father made his fortune in patent medicine. The elaborate family home, Fulford Place, is now a museum.

A bellyflop contest at Brockville.

The central waterfront of Brockville was occupied by factories. Huge supplies of coal and oil were brought to the waterfront by freighters, and flames shot up the smokestack of the foundry. The rail lines were here, including the long underground railway tunnel that children loved to explore on Sundays when the trains weren't running. Because there was no place for the smoke to escape in the tunnel, the engine emerged pushing a big cloud in front of it.

Booze was more easily available in the United States than in Canada — except during Prohibition — and so people from Brockville took the ferry to Morristown to drink. In exchange, the people from Morristown, who didn't have to go looking for taverns, came to Brockville to see western movies. The ferry service operated until the 1950s and local people can still remember back to the 1930s when the ferry whistle was the signal that the boat was arriving. In the wintertime, people from Brockville could snowshoe across the ice in twenty minutes. The ice made it easy to socialize across the border. That's how many marriages between Canadians and the Americans came about — facilitated by a frozen river. When the bridges were built across the St. Lawrence River, upriver and downriver of Brockville, crossing here became more inconvenient and these romances less frequent.

BLOCKHOUSE
ISLAND PARK

This waterfront park is a good vantage point. It's located where the river channel narrows and the freighters come so close they almost seem to dance with the sailboats. This piece of land was central to the history of Brockville. A hospital was established on the island during the cholera epidemic of 1832 to quarantine immigrants who carried the disease up the river by boat. Later, during the 1837 Rebellion, the blockhouse that gave the island its name was built to protect the town from the threat of the rebels. Then, in the 1850s, to form a network with the shipping on the river, a railway was built to Brockville. At that time Blockhouse Island had become an industrial centre for the community and a railway depot. When the railway tunnel was excavated under the city in the 1850s, the earth was used to connect the island to the mainland. The island is thus no longer a true island, although the people of the city still like to call it one. On a clear day the bridge downriver at Johnstown can be seen from the park.

❧ OTHER ATTRACTIONS ❧

The Brockville Museum

St. Brendan's Church, Rockport.

THE THOUSAND
ISLANDS PARKWAY

THE TWILIGHT OF THE GODS

THE PARKWAY

N EXT TO A BRIDGE or a ferry, this stretch of road between Brockville and Gananoque gives the best and longest unobstructed view of the river and the islands, with two beaches, a number of lookout stops and several old river towns along the way. Along the road, particularly in the marshes near Mallorytown Landing, are fishing grounds of the great blue heron and other water birds. The birds gather during migration in the spring and the fall. At twilight, the broad gulf of water goes through a series of heavenly purple hues, and you might just see a ragged old heron standing in the middle of it all on his favourite rock.

CHIMNEY ISLAND

Even small islands like Chimney Island have their own rich histories. Chimney Island wasn't large enough to farm, but a historian, Don Ross, tells the story of how two Metis hunters and a French-Canadian built separate cabins on the island in 1799. Everything might have worked well had the French-Canadian not upset the balance among the three inhabitants by bringing his young Indian wife to the island. It was an inflammable situation — three men on an isolated island with one beautiful woman. Before long, the island was set on fire and the French-Canadian was murdered.

131

Local people believe that the two Metis took the wife to share and killed the French-Canadian, leaving his ghost stuck on the island all this time.

During the War of 1812, with a military garrison stationed on the mainland near here, a blockhouse was built on the island to protect the supply route along the northern channel. The blockhouse crumbled, but its chimney stood for years as a monument to the vanished inhabitants. One legend says that an old woman kept the lone chimney in good repair because a fortune teller told her she would die when it fell down.

MALLORYTOWN LANDING

The village of Mallorytown was founded by the Mallory family and other United Empire Loyalists who were fleeing the American Revolution. Mallorytown was divided between the old centre of industry on the old main road a few kilometres through the rock to the north, and the port on the river, called Mallorytown Landing.

A hundred years ago the village of Mallorytown was so industrious that it was the site of a glassworks, a brickyard, and a cheese factory. It was also home, in the 1830s, to the Mallorytown Total Abstinence Society, which would have been kept busy with the number of distilleries along the river. Historian Ruth McKenzie gives a good account of the industry of the Mallorys. She says that, in the 1850s, a man named David Mallory owned one of the many brickyards in the area that produced, from the red clay soil, the characteristic orange-red Mallorytown brick. Another Mallory, named Andrew, ran the glassworks in the mid-1800s that made a bluish-green glass used for bottles and paperweights. And yet another Mallory, named Amasa, ran a cheese factory in the 1870s that made cheese good enough to win a prize at the Chicago World's Fair in 1893.

132

BROWN'S BAY WRECK

This is a Parks Canada display of a large gunboat typical of the War of 1812 era. The gunboats carried small cannons that could rip you to pieces if you got in their way. This one was built in Kingston in 1817 and was retrieved from the bottom of the river where it had lain undisturbed for more than a century. The gunboat display is situated at one of the nicest sand beaches on the St. Lawrence River, at Mallorytown Landing.

JORSTADT CASTLE
(1896–1904)

The glimmer of the red tile roof of Jorstadt Castle, like a mirage in the heat of the summer, is just visible in the distance from the Mallorytown Landing area. The island and the castle, sitting in an open stretch of water, take the brunt of the wind and the storms. At night, it's a dark stretch of water. Some people still use the old name the river pilots gave the island, Dark Island. The Indians, also recognizing the isolation of the island, called it Lone Star. The castle was built at the turn of the century by the owner of the Singer Sewing Machine Company. It's made of red granite and has a five-storey clock tower with Westminster chimes. On a calm night the chimes can be heard as far away as Chippewa Bay.

Jorstadt Castle, like Boldt Castle, sums up the period from the 1880s to 1910, when the Thousand Islands went through a time of wealth and prosperity. One island, near Chippewa Bay, was given the name Ragnarok in the 1890s. Ragnarok is the Norse myth of the Twilight of the Gods, the big, final battle where the gods are annihilated in a battle with the ancient monsters of the world. During the early 1900s, the Bourne family, who built the castle, rode the river in a gondola imported from Venice, with a boatman dressed as a gondolier. In Victorian style, the wealthy ladies living in summer homes on the islands went to tea in white gloves, driven by uniformed boatmen. Meanwhile, the farm wives fed the animals, trapped muskrats, and tended big families.

The wealth in the islands reached its peak with the construction of Boldt Castle and Jorstadt Castle. It then took the kind of turn downwards that David Holdt called "economic evolution." The castles became economic millstones around the necks of their owners. Boldt Castle was eventually sold to the Thousand Islands Bridge Authority. Meanwhile, those with less money did better through this period. The families who had purchased the cheap, poor farmland on the islands in the 1800s, or the castoff property along the shoreline, left an inheritance of valuable land for their descendants.

In the 1960s, Jorstadt Castle was bought by a wealthy Canadian evangelist, Dr. Harold Martin. Martin was regarded with suspicion by the river people. When he originally bought the castle through a non-profit religious corporation, there were stories about him carrying suitcases full of money to the island. But that sounds a lot like the same old feverish speculation about the buried gold of Billa Larue or the loot on the steamboat *Sir Robert Peel*.

LARUE'S CREEK

Billa Larue logged trees on Hill Island and then established a mill that supplied grain to the troops in the War of 1812. Like Joel Stone, the founder of the town of Gananoque, Larue seized on the creek as a way to win money and influence in the community. Larue dammed the creek and built a mill, which became the basis of a fortune that later inspired people to speculate about buried gold. Hunting for buried gold was a popular pastime along the river a hundred years ago. People came looking for it at night with divining rods and one group was scared away by cows they mistook for phantoms. There was also the rumour of a gold mine in the area. When Larue died, he left his wife the bed and forty pounds a year, provided she moved out of their house so that their daughter could live there. The small family graveyard nearby has been turned into a historical site. Larue's tombstone not only records his date of birth and his death, but the number of years, months and days of his life, like the final tally in a businessman's ledger book.

ROCKPORT

Rockport was a perfect spot along the river for steamboats to stop for fuel wood, and so, in the 1800s, a community grew up around the piles of wood. Before long there was a cheese factory for the farms. Craftsmen built skiffs, small boat engines, and the occasional steamboat. The farmers on the islands nearby paddled around the river to sell their chickens and vegetables. The cheese from the cheese factory was loaded on steamboats and sent to Montreal. From there it was shipped to Great Britain.

Typical of those who originally settled here was Michael O'Connor, driven out of Ireland by hard times in the late 1800s. He settled nearby and farmed the tough, rocky soil until he and his family moved into the village. In time, his son Manville started working as a boy on one of the river steamboats. When the First World War broke out, Manville O'Connor was so keen to see action on the seas that he joined the United States Navy. He was still a Canadian, which was a problem, although people along the river had always ignored the border as a dividing line. Manville had a crooked judge across the river in Alexandria Bay prepare some false papers for him. Later, he married an Irish immigrant in New York City and returned to Rockport to raise a family. He was buried near Rockport, still a Canadian citizen, but with an American flag draped over his coffin and the symbol of the U.S. Navy on his gravestone.

For years, a gap between the large islands made it easy to travel back and forth between Rockport and Alexandria Bay, on the American side. That connection brought the two communities closer together, affecting their growth and character. In the early 1900s, two ferries, the *Roosevelt* and the *General Hancock*, ran back and forth, until the river froze for the season and barred their way. The people of Rockport took the ferry to Alexandria Bay to have the dentist there pull their teeth. When Alexandria Bay needed a jail, the town hired a boozing stone mason from the Canadian side of the river. It's said that the workman got drunk after he finished the jail and became the first customer. The last day of the ferry run in September was a celebration in the village, drawing a crowd to watch the boat leave. The cheese factory burned down because of a hot cinder from the same ferry. The day the cheese factory burned, a new metal roof, which would have been impervious to cinders, was waiting to be installed.

The location of Rockport on the river was convenient during the Prohibition era, when local people took booze across the river at night to Alexandria Bay and Chippewa Bay. Some of the booze was hidden under floor boards in the cheese factory. There's also a story about a female smuggler from the American side of the river. She smuggled by rowing her skiff back and forth with her baby nestled in it. Smuggling on the river was a dangerous proposition. It meant taking the risk of working on the river at night and in cold weather. The river often took the lives of the smugglers. Manville O'Connor once found the body of a smuggler washed up on shore in the springtime.

Frank Fitzsimmons, the customs agent at this time, had an office upstairs in the general store. He and his wife ran a tourism home called the Hickory Lodge. The guests, in their neat, white flannel clothes, sat on the porch to enjoy the elegant mood of the islands. The lodge, like many buildings along the river, eventually burned down. Fitzsimmons is remembered for the advice that he gave every newlywed couple coming off the ferry. He said: "Don't ever both get mad at the same time."

LOOKING AROUND THE ROCK

There's still enough rock left in Rockport to understand how the village got its name. The place was originally called Stoney Town, but that was changed to the more dignified title of Rockport. The big rock that gave Rockport its name was blasted, according to a story in the village, because some of the residents thought it blocked their view of the river.

The village, though small, is a nice shady spot to stretch your legs. You can still get a sense of the quiet place where children wandered years ago, picking grapes from the vines that had wound themselves around Mr. Root's tree next to the river, or plucking apples from the orchard, farther along. In those days, if the children were still hungry, they could also get curds from the cheese factory.

ST. BRENDAN'S ROMAN CATHOLIC CHURCH
(1891)

Built by Irish settlers on a cliff overlooking the St. Lawrence River, this church was named after the Irish monk, St. Brendan, the patron saint of sailors. The stained-glass windows were rowed to the church forty-five kilometres from Kingston. A large white statue of the Virgin Mary holding the infant Jesus was placed on the cliff in front of the church in 1919 and has served as a kind of beacon for boaters ever since.

Drifting in a boat at Landon's Bay, east of Gananoque.

GANANOQUE

GANANOQUE

G ANANOQUE LOOKS reasonably tame today, but there was a time when wolves howled in the woods outside town. In those days, the late 1700s, defending a place like Gananoque meant more than protecting it from raids by Americans. It meant fortifying the people against the wilderness. At that time nature was so bountiful, it was almost overwhelming. The woods were full of bears and the swamps crawled with muskrats. The flocks of ducks were so thick that when they flew the noise of their wings sounded like thunder. The wolves — which have since disappeared from southern Ontario — killed sheep, calves and the occasional cow. They could be shot from the doorstep and were said to dig up the graves of infants. Not far away, the town of Kingston wasn't much different, with fighting pigs and people who kept wild deer in paddocks for the meat.

This is the type of frontier that the founder of Gananoque, Joel Stone, encountered when he came here in 1792. Stone was a typical settler in the Thousand Islands. A Connecticut Yankee, he was caught up in a rebellion he opposed, the American Revolution, and fled to Canada as a United Empire Loyalist. The year after Stone settled at the Gananoque River, the wolf bounty was established in the province, and Stone himself offered ten dollars for every wolf shot in the settlement. He also offered twenty-five

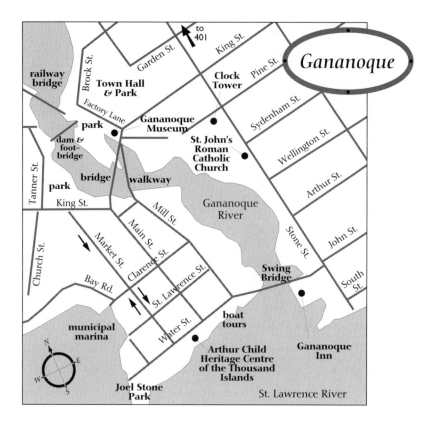

cents for each crow shot on his side of the Gananoque River, and twenty cents a head on the other side.

Stone seized upon the Gananoque River — named by the Iroquois, who camped here and on the islands — and the St. Lawrence River as a way to make money for himself. He saw the potential for mills and a port and even charged a fee to ferry people and animals across the Gananoque River. Following his insight, the town developed into a river port. Lumber was floated down the Gananoque River by Stone's son-in-law. Mills, and later, factories, spread along on the Gananoque River, and made use of a trading ship that Stone built here. In the 1820s, a monstrous flour mill took grain that came from the west in schooners, and sent the flour down the river in Durham boats. In the years that followed, Gananoque grew as an industrial town, making bolts, spoons, nails, steamboat fittings, rakes, shovels and carriages. By the 1870s, there were forty-nine mills and factories in town.

The industries in town, which started with water power, shifted easily to electricity with the creation of the Gananoque Light and Power Company. The company was started in 1885, and so that year the lights first went on in Gananoque. The private company still supplies power to the town. It has partial control of the Gananoque River and manages nine dams on the series of lakes that drain into the river and the Rideau Canal.

Gananoque's military history goes back to the War of 1812, when the town's size and position on the river made it vulnerable to attacks. At that time, the settlement was raided by Yankees, led by the troublemaker Captain Benjamin Forsyth, and the bridge across the Gananoque River was destroyed.

After the Yankee raid, Gananoque became the site of a navy gunboat station, defending the British supply line along the north channel of the river. The British decided to protect Gananoque and the St. Lawrence River by building a blockhouse. Unfortunately, it was way too far up the Gananoque River to be any use. Gananoque wasn't much of a prize for the Americans anyway, but it was a good place to launch a diversionary attack.

One of those diversions came during the 1837 Rebellion. The American sympathizers of the rebels planned to cross the ice to Gananoque on the birthday of George Washington. It was part of a master plan to take Kingston, and the attack here was probably intended to draw troops out of the fort. Then the prisoners would be released from the prison in Kingston and overwhelm the town. The attack on Kingston was expected for

months, but it was Elizabeth Barnett, an American teaching school in
Gananoque, who pinpointed Gananoque as the first stage. Barnett crossed
the ice before the renegades and warned the townsfolk of troops amassing
nearby on Hickory Island, where a widow lived by herself.

Some people in Gananoque think the school teacher saved Upper
Canada and has been unjustly ignored by history. Others give the credit for
the rout to the disintegration of the American forces, fuelled by the sol-
diers' disgust at their disorderly commander, Rensselaer Van Rensselaer.
Van Rensselaer was the son of the general who faced Brock at the battle of
Queenston Heights. One of those taken prisoner told the British that the
Americans had refused to attack Gananoque and got drunk on the island
instead. Another story says that the Americans were frightened away when
they captured a spy who told them the troops were waiting for them in
Gananoque.

As for Barnett, she fell in love with one of the soldiers that was sent to
Gananoque when she sounded the alarm. The two married a month later
and settled outside town. Barnett gave birth to eleven children and died at
ninety-two years of age.

After all the years that have passed, Gananoque still feels like a town on
the edge of the frontier. The townsfolk measure the seasons by watching
the ice come and go on the river. And the crows that the founder of the
town wanted eliminated are still cawing from the trees. One of their
favourite spots is the Catholic cemetery. "I'd like to shoot them all," says one
of the officers on the town police force. "They like the cemetery because
there's nobody to bother them."

GANANOQUE MUSEUM
(CIRCA 1840s)

The building was originally constructed as a hotel and went through a
number of proper British names. First the hotel was called the Albion Hote

and later, in 1901, the Victoria Hotel. A few years later the building was converted into the office of the Jones Shovel Company, which, as the historian Ruth McKenzie says, supplied shovels for three wars. Now it has been converted into a museum. Included in the collection is a Link trainer, which is one of the dummy aircraft cockpits built in town to train pilots during the Second World War. Spending taxpayers' money on the museum was once described as "pouring sand down a rat hole," during a feud between local historians. However, the museum has been working to improve its collection.

GANANOQUE TOWN HALL
(1831)

The Gananoque Town Hall started as the home of John McDonald, one of the founders of Gananoque. It was constructed of bricks likely brought across the ocean from Great Britain as the ballast of a ship. The building was used later as a court office, library, and jail, and is now the town hall. The council meets upstairs in what once was the ballroom. The mayor's office was the master bedroom. On the top floor is a tiny replica of an old schoolroom.

CLOCK TOWER
(1903)

This bow-sided brick structure was built as a gift to the town from its bridge-building resident, Charles Macdonald. It was designed by the American architect Franklin T. Lent and has a clock that chimes every hour. For years, the chimes have irritated sleepers to the point where they get out of bed, sneak up the stairs inside the tower, and stop the mechanism. The tall interior of the structure was used years ago to hang the hoses of the fire department until they dried.

Lent designed a number of cottages and buildings on both sides of the river. He was a quiet, meditative man who fished and painted on the river. One of his paintings shows a scene of the moon rising over the water from the vantage point of a small island near Gananoque called Wee Rocks. Lent designed and built a cottage on Wee Rocks, with a fanciful curved bridge connecting it to a minuscule island. The two tiny islands were once called The Sisters. The place is now called La Vignette. Lent also designed a villa on Howe Island with panels painted with scenes from the story of Hiawatha.

ST. JOHN THE EVANGELIST ROMAN CATHOLIC CHURCH
(1889–1891)

Late in the 1800s, the Roman Catholics in Gananoque decided to build a huge, Gothic church that seemed to fit the ambitions of a large city better than a small town like Gananoque. Most of the buildings in Gananoque were made of granite, sandstone, or humble ballast brick, but not this church. It was built of limestone on a cliff along the Gananoque River, with eight hundred and thirty seats for the thriving Roman Catholic population. The town was incorporated during that period, in 1890, with a population of 3,600. The limestone for the building was brought from nearby Howe Island.

THE WATERFRONT AND OLD PORT TOWN

The development of Gananoque reflected its relationship to the waterfront. Originally, the settlement was clustered around Water Street, near where the Public Utility Commission building is now, with water-powered mills along the Gananoque River. Then, as the mills became steel plants, the settlement began to move up the Gananoque River.

During this period, the influence of the St. Lawrence was still strong. Gananoque was linked with Clayton in the United States by ferry service from the early 1800s. The town was also located along one of the shipping routes. In the 1850s, several lighthouses were built on islands nearby to help the ships on the river. One of the lighthouses had a library to lend books to people on the islands. The lighthouses were tended over the years by townsfolk. One of these lighthouse keepers, Poppy Glover, had a round friendly face and wore a vest with a watch and chain everywhere he went, even in a boat on the river. He rowed to the lighthouse in his St. Lawrence skiff. After breathing the fresh air of the river all his life, Poppy Glover lived to be ninety-five years old.

Gananoque didn't have shipyards on the scale of Kingston and Clayton, but like any town on the river it still made a noble effort at building ships. One of those, the two-hundred-and-fifty-ton steamboat *William IV*, was built here in the 1830s. The *William IV* was launched late in the season for a run from Brockville to Niagara. This was the ship that the poet and novelist Susanna Moodie took up the river. Moodie joined the new ship in Prescott, where it was packed with Irish immigrants, and she didn't get much enjoyment out of the Thousand Islands because of the combination of a gale outside her door and a wild Irishman who sang through the night. Moodie missed seeing the Thousand Islands entirely. She was driven back to her room by the storm and wrote, "I returned wet and disappointed to my berth."

During the 1837 Rebellion, the *William IV* was used to bring soldiers and artillery to the main battle at Prescott. A few years later, on Halloween, the ship was breached by strong seas in Lake Ontario and had to be run aground to save it and the passengers. After that, the *William IV* worked as a tugboat. Finally, having served its time, the engines were removed for another ship and the *William IV* was sunk in the graveyard of ships at Garden Island, near Kingston.

In the 1900s, ships were losing the battle to the railroads, and cars were challenging the rails. Then along came the improvements to highways that changed Gananoque forever. Merchants clustered around the main road and moved even farther inland, until the town abandoned the St. Lawrence River almost entirely. And yet the Gananoque River remained an influence on the character of the community.

These days, Gananoque is struggling to reestablish its connection to the river. For many years, the town ignored the St. Lawrence and let itself be shaped by the demands of roads and cars. Recently, in an attempt to reclaim its waterfront for public use, the town built a public marina, a park on a small peninsula jutting out into the river, and a museum. The museum, called the Arthur Child Heritage Centre of the Thousand Islands, is on the waterfront beside the dock for the boat tours.

GANANOQUE INN AND THE SWING BRIDGE

The Gananoque Inn was originally a carriage factory, built around 1885, and converted to an inn a few years later. The narrow bridge that spans the nearby Gananoque River was built in 1894 as a railway bridge to supply the carriage factory. The bridge was made to swing, to allow coal barges to come up the Gananoque River to the factories that were once there. The bridge is still operable, thanks to political pressure on the town council. For decades, fishing guides from Gananoque have worked out of the inn. The present inn has maintained the original style of architecture, although much of the original building was destroyed in a fire in 1907. In the early 1900s, the inn had its own small steamboat, the *Antelope,* to give tours of the islands and pick up guests from the other side of the river.

THE BATEAU CHANNEL

Highway 2, the road between Gananoque and Kingston, runs beside a quiet stretch of water known as the Bateau Channel and past a quiet island called

Howe. The people who built the road took a relatively straight and logical route. However, the result was to distance travellers from the river. The road has made people oblivious to the life of the river that lies hidden behind trees and a wide gulf of land.

In the 1700s, people travelled the channel here in a type of cargo boat, twelve metres long, known as a bateau. The boats carried people and supplies up the river to Kingston, making stops along the way at inns and farm houses. The bateau was moved by sails and oars and carried provisions of rum to keep the sailors warm and comfortable. Some of the sailors were French-Canadians. Others came from the naval forces that came during the War of 1812. After bringing people up the river, the boats returned with cargoes of flour and furs. The same type of boat was used to carry British troops and prisoners captured during the War of 1812.

After the settlers came to the area in the late 1700s and early 1800s, the first tourists arrived. They were Victorians, like Charles Dickens, and considered themselves great travellers and travel writers. Some of the Victorians loved the scenery here; others thought it was boring and pointless. Some complained that the sailors were drunk, and that their fellow passengers were rude. Some of them were disappointed that they couldn't see castles, as they would on the Rhine. According to them, there were too many islands, and too much of anything puts one to sleep. One British traveller, Edward Talbot, found the peace of the river in the 1820s a "cheerless solitude." The islands needed builders, he said, "to redeem them from their unproductiveness." Victorians were the kind of people who enjoyed being out of touch with reality. In the mid-1800s, the river, still a wilderness, threatened their way of thinking. As city dwellers, they found it contradictory to their ideas of stimulation and vitality. And so Lady Durham, who travelled the Thousand Islands in 1838 just a few years before Dickens, thought it good mostly for pirates, with "nothing grand" in itself. In the late 1800s, the Victorians built castles and grand hotels on the islands to make the wilderness fit their notions of magnificence.

The head of a moose is embedded in the stone fireplace of Nokomis Lodge, Howe Island.

HOWE ISLAND

There are two ferries that operate from Howe Island, and, if you're not in a hurry, a detour across the island can be a nice diversion. The island, a township unto itself, has its own volunteer fire department and looks after one of the island's two ferries. The township staff plows the roads in the wintertime. For ambulances and police, the islanders have to rely on people from the mainland.

The island, like others on the river, was once good grazing for sheep. In the late 1800s, you would have seen more sheep than people. At that time, the island had about four hundred people and six hundred sheep. The people here were mostly Irish Roman Catholics and their main crop was wool. The oldest residents remember the days when the islanders didn't use money. They bartered for store goods with milk, eggs and wool. Today there are few farms and practically no sheep. The winter population is about four hundred and, with all of the cottages, the number triples in the summertime.

On the north side of the island is a bay so large that it looks like a channel through two islands. Years ago, this was a perfect spot to trap muskrats in the spring. In a good season, a trapper could catch between one hundred and three hundred muskrats. One of the best trappers, from Gananoque, trapped five hundred muskrats here in a season. The muskrats were skinned and the pelts dried. The pelts were then sold to the owner of a grocery store in Gananoque. According to one farmer from the island, there were thieves who used to take the muskrats out of the traps. They'd cut a leg off and leave it in the trap to make it look as though the animal had broken free by itself. At the end of the trapping season, the trappers who came to the island from Gananoque held a big feast and served muskrat stew. The islanders themselves didn't eat the muskrats they trapped. The muskrats reminded them of rats, which isn't far-fetched, since they belong to the same family of rodents. The trappers took the meat home to eat and said it tasted wonderful.

The islands, particularly those without ferries, have lost much of their population since the 1950s. However, there are a few people who live on the islands year round. They think that life on an island gives them something they can't find elsewhere. There's no denying that life on an island was tough years ago. As one old farmer from Howe Island says, if the hail storms weren't flattening his crops, it was either too dry for them to grow, or too wet. But these people like being away from the noise and confusion of the cities. On the river, they can forget the silly distractions of humanity and absorb the big, open, soulful space of the St. Lawrence. As they say, "Kingston is crowded; sometimes you like to come home where it's peaceful and quiet."

RIVER RATS, MUSKRATS AND OTHER RODENT LORE

FOR YEARS, PEOPLE on both sides of the river have been calling themselves river rats. It's an old term, going back in North America to the 1880s. At first, the words were meant to be derogatory. Rats were creepy. They carried disease. They were wicked and cunning. But the river people took the term river rat in a different sense. The term was a way to distinguish themselves from city people. Like the big water rodents, the beaver and the muskrat, the river was their territory.

Other cultures have cherished the rodent. In India, the rat was revered; for the ancient Egyptians, in the *Egyptian Book of the Dead*, the animal was part of a formula for praising a god as a provider; and the Ojibwa made the muskrat the hero of their story of creation. In the story the world sinks beneath a flood. Three animals are given the task of diving down to the bottom and recovering the mud that will start a new world. The first three to try are obvious choices — beaver, loon, and otter — and they fail. Then the muskrat tries. He brings up the mud that magically starts a new world. In the process the muskrat sacrifices his life and dies. Out of a reward for his heroic effort, his kind is allowed to multiply, which explains, according to the story, why there is such a natural proliferation of muskrats.

The muskrat is the most common rat on the river. People in the city of Kingston, near the old swamps, sometimes see a muskrat scuttling across the road. They mistake it for a common rat and think that the rats are growing bigger. In fact, the muskrats are the same size, but their numbers are growing. Muskrats were an easy supply of food for the Indians and the first white settlers. Archaeologists excavated an Iroquois village in the area that was inhabited before contact with the first European explorers and found that muskrats were at the top of the menu behind deer, bear, and racoon. The study of the excavation noted that when Jacques Cartier arrived later at the lower St. Lawrence he considered muskrat meat a delicacy. Centuries later, folks now living in the Thousand Islands remember eating muskrat meat as children. A few of the remaining trappers still eat muskrat meat. They say that they prefer the meat to that of an animal raised in a dirty barnyard. They have fond memories of trapping muskrats as children. They were intrigued by the idea of matching wits with such a cunning animal and catching it. During the hard years of the Depression, trapping muskrats was an easy way to make good money. The children would skip school to mind their traps. They idolized the men who were trappers and knew the world of nature. The river rats were their heroes.

It takes some passion to become a river rat. It means long hours spent on the river ignoring the comforts and distractions of the towns and cities. But there is a sense of honour and reward in knowing the river well and being able to cope with its difficulties. The river rats of the Thousand Islands have adapted to their world, unlike those who try to make the world adapt to them.

THE INDIANS OF THE THOUSAND ISLANDS

T HE THOUSAND ISLANDS was once a place where the Mohawks, Oneidas, and Mississauga Ojibwa came for visits in the summertime. They hunted, fished and set up camps on the islands and at the mouths of rivers, where the fish spawned. Much like the settlers from Europe who followed them — at first hermits and people who could afford only the poorest land — they treated the islands as a kind of shadowy borderland and not land that anybody would want to possess.

In the late 1700s, the British, who did not share the same concept of holding and possessing land as the Indians, wanted the territory along the upper St. Lawrence River. It was useful to them as a place to settle their allies from the American Revolution. Those allies, besides the United Empire Loyalists and people who fought on the British side, also included the Mohawks from the Iroquois Six Nations, and a few slaves that the white people brought with them. The British gave the Mohawk clan mother, Molly Brant, her request for land and a house at the British settlement at Cataraqui, where Kingston was established. And yet, Sir Frederick Haldimand, the governor of Canada at the time, acceded rather ungraciously to what he saw as the excessive demands of the woman. He said that her request amounted to "the lesser evil," with the British saving money because of her influence over the Indians.

153

Under Haldimand, the land around the old French Fort at Cataraqui was purchased from the Mississauga Ojibwa, in 1783 and 1784, together with shoreline property along the St. Lawrence River and Lake Ontario. Haldimand even boasted of how the Indians had been bamboozled out of their land "for an inconsiderable sum." The British took the property for a few pieces of cloth and some guns. It wasn't until much later, in 1856, that the Mississaugas surrendered the islands on the Canadian side of the river in a trust agreement. By then the Mississaugas had left the area. They had embraced Methodism in the mid-1820s and become part of an ill-fated experiment in farming on tiny Grape Island, on the Bay of Quinte, near Belleville. After that, the government moved them to the Rice Lake area, which had the consolations of good farm land and good muskrat trapping.

And yet, even through the mid-1800s, the settlers from Europe still felt the presence of the people who came before them. The settlers came to admire the skill and daring of these people on the rapids between Prescott and Montreal, recalling how Champlain, exploring the river in 1611, was amazed at their cleverness in shooting the rough water in fragile canoes. Later, the Indians became pilots, and navigated the huge timber rafts and steamboats through the rapids. Some people in the Morrisburg area still remember the days before the St. Lawrence Seaway when the Indians rode the rapids and returned home by the railway. The train was called The Moccasin because the Indians left their wet shoes to dry on the heaters, with the sweet perfume of deerhide filling the air.

SMUGGLING DURING PROHIBITION (1920–1933)

T HE RIVER COMMUNITY was already rebellious, in a way, long before Prohibition arrived in the United States at the beginning of the 1920s. The islanders and the people of the river towns began to smuggle as soon as the two countries set up trade barriers. Throughout the War of 1812, they didn't bend to the political demands of the time, instead keeping their old ties and smuggling when they wished. Almost everything imaginable was smuggled across the river, from potash and lumber, to cattle and horses. Prohibition simply gave the river community a fresh opportunity to prove that the border area was a wide gulf where a boat that didn't want to be found couldn't be found.

One of the last remaining smugglers from the Prohibition era is Chuck Thomas of Alexandria Bay. In the 1920s and 1930s, Alexandria Bay — or what Thomas calls Little Chicago — was the centre of smuggling in the islands. "You couldn't believe the things that happened," says Thomas. "Cripes, someone would go and get a load of whisky and you'd never hear from him again. About twenty years later he'd show up." Thomas made over two hundred trips hauling contraband booze between the Bay and secluded Canadian spots such as Ivy Lea and Rockport. He says that he was never caught once. He knew every little bay and narrow channel. The smuggler could slip his boat under the shroud of a weeping willow tree that hung over the river and disappear from sight as though he had erased himself from the Earth.

The flow of illicit booze was controlled, the old smuggler says, by mobsters in Utica and Syracuse. The smugglers would take contraband through the array of channels between the islands. Catching the smugglers on the river was so difficult that it was easier for the officers of the law to wait until the smugglers touched the mainland and lost their advantage.

Smuggling flourished in several places simultaneously. At the upper end of the river, the smuggling was concentrated around Kingston and the nearby islands of Wolfe and Simcoe, and at a bleak fishing island in Lake Ontario called the Main Ducks. One of preferred routes was a large sweep out into the lake where the noise of the boats was lost in the open space. This overcame the disadvantage of the islands, which offered a labyrinth of channels, but also amplified the sound of the boats. Some boats were outfitted with underwater exhaust pipes to muffle their passage.

Smugglers were popular in the cities. They would spend lavishly, and give folks money and children candy. The most popular of the bootleggers, such as Kingston's eccentric Dollar Bill, did the same, and were also well liked for their generosity. While the rest of the continent suffered through the Depression, the river people made good money by breaking a law that few felt was legitimate anyway.

Of course, in Little Chicago, there were stories of snitches whose arms were broken, or independent smugglers whose homes were burned by mobsters, or even the odd shoot-out on the river. One smuggler's boat sank to the bottom of the river in a blaze of gunfire. Another had the back of his boat so badly shot with holes that he had to keep the speed up all the way back to Simcoe Island to keep the water from coming in. For the most part, the smugglers saw themselves as part of the common folk, sometimes victimized by people with power and money from the cities, and restricted by a senseless bureaucracy. For this moment at least, they were the ones in control, on a river that they knew best, and they had the complete backing of the community.

One sign of the local support came in a letter to the editor of a newspaper in 1922 from the owner of the Thousand Island House and the Crossman Hotel. He criticized the local newspaper for running a story about bootlegging in the community. "I personally would greatly appreciate it if you will keep the soft pedal on such matters," he said. His two hotels offered a good supply of booze during these years. Ten years later, not much had changed. During a raid at a bar in Alexandria Bay in 1932, two agents of the law were kicked and beaten by the crowd and the tires of their car slashed. The raid ended in the arrest of five residents, but the officers had to be rescued by the state troopers. They returned two days later with more firepower, and the local newspaper gloated that the incidents meant a lot of free advertising for Alexandria Bay.

Most of the stories from the smuggling communities are told at the expense of the police. The smugglers had all kinds of ways to hide the booze in cars and could throw their loads over the side of a boat if the law was too close. In boats, the smugglers either had hidden compartments or packaged the bottles in unusual ways. According to one story, even fish were used to conceal the smuggling. Bottles were stuffed inside large fish to get them across the border. On the train that crossed the border from Montreal to New York, people who wanted to bring liquor back would tie a shoelace around a bottle and hang it out the window. Anybody who needed to get rid of the evidence just opened the window. Sometimes this trick backfired, because the railway workers outside the train would steal the bottles. At Ogdensburg, the ferry that brought the trains across the river was used by the smugglers as a place to conceal contraband. One time the circus was late getting to Ogdensburg because the officers were so busy hunting down the concealed booze. Some of the bottles were hidden in the tiger cages. Another time a cab driver got booze across the border by flashing a fake police badge.

And yet, the agents developed their own tricks for catching the smugglers. An easy tactic was to follow a drunk back to the source, since drunks are terribly bad at keeping a secret. Another giveaway was the sound of clinking bottles under the clothes of the ferry passengers.

During Prohibition, the United States Border Patrol was stationed at Cape Vincent, across the river from such trouble spots as Kingston and Wolfe Island. From there the agents covered the district on the American side as far downriver as Alexandria Bay. Henry Denner, from a family of ship captains who owned a hundred islands in the river, was in charge of the station. After working for border patrol, Denner became the sheriff in the county and kept his pet raccoons, skunks, and deer in the county jail yard. Denner was battered and shot at by the smugglers and was wounded in a gun battle. One of his brothers, who also worked for the border patrol, walked across the ice from Morristown to Brockville to trail a suspect as far as Montreal. The smuggling was particularly easy across the ice, which was one more reason why smuggling was widespread.

The Canadians used the border to their advantage. One enterprising man kept a supply of liquor on an island just inside the Canadian side of the border. Anybody who wanted a bottle just called out to him over the water and he rowed the order across. He was caught by one of the Denner brothers who simply called out an order and waited until the man rowed into his arms.

Some of the booze is still believed to be lying on the bottom of the river or hidden in secret caches, like pots of gold. Once in a while, some-body claims to have found an old supply. One day in the 1950s — or so the story goes — a work crew discovered an old cache of liquor, from Prohibition days, near Ivy Lea. The booze was in a crevice of a rock down by the river. The men started drinking it on a Friday and kept going through the whole weekend.

Like everybody else, wealthy people and government officials snubbed the prohibition laws. The wealthy people bought islands on the Canadian side of the river so that they could keep drinking through the dry times. According to one story, an official of the Canadian government was caught trying to sell contraband booze in a drug store in Alexandria Bay in 1920. With a suitcase loaded with Scotch, he was making his pitch near an immigration agent who had stopped at the store on his way home. Some law officials from the United States were taking bribes, which led to the dismissal of border patrol agents in the Ogdensburg area in 1927.

Today, on the river, there are whispers of this or that fortune made a generation or two ago in contraband, and, in spite of the numbers of years that have passed, people are still reluctant to tell all the tales. In Alexandria Bay, you can get a drink at the Bootlegger's Cafe. You can also walk the streets where the booze flowed in illegal establishments called Blind Pigs and where the presence of an officer was known the moment he put his foot in town. During prohibition, Boldt Castle, across from the Bay, was an empty shell of granite. Abandoned and left unfinished in 1904, it was an ideal spot for hiding liquor. Boats making smuggling runs from Canada would hide on the north side of the island until dark, and then head for a nearby bay or creek, to unload the booze into cars and trucks.

COUNTING ISLANDS

EVER SINCE PEOPLE have been coming to the Thousand Islands they've been trying to decide how many islands there are here, which is like trying to count the stars in the sky or grains of sand on the beach. The French explorers started the number game when they gave the name Les Mille Iles to this part of the St. Lawrence River. It was a reasonable guess about the number of islands, particularly since, like all people in a hurry, the French didn't have time to stop and count islands. Others, even among the early French travelers, didn't believe there really were a thousand islands. A skeptical Jesuit passing through the area in the 1720s said that he thought there must be five hundred islands. The Jesuit was wrong, dead wrong, because there are more than a thousand islands. Depending on what you consider an island, a more or less reliable number is 1,860. But, of course, the name the Thousand Islands sounds more elegant.

ENDNOTES

1   In his biography of Dickens, Fred Kaplan explores this idea, with comments such as, "The edge, the frontier, the open spaces, seemed to him empty or, even worse, savage." Fred Kaplan. *Dickens: A Biography*. (New York: Avon Books, 1988), pp. 137–138.

2   Neil K. MacLennan, "City Hall Today," in Ian E. Wilson, ed., *Kingston City Hall*. (Kingston: The City of Kingston, 1974), p. 24.

3   Dickens's apparent reservations, running contrary to his public enthusiasm, were expressed in a letter to the staff keeper of the prison. Bill Harpell says he saw the letter while he worked in the prison in the 1950s. The letter was sent to the dump along with a lot of old papers. See my article, "Dickens letter found and lost," *The Kingston Whig-Standard*, November 26, 1994.

4   Nelie Horton Casler, *Cape Vincent and Its History* (Watertown, N.Y.: Hungerford-Holbrook Co., 1906).

5   The information about Kepler comes from an interview with his grandson, William C. Hartman, and Hartman's book, *The Legendary Wit and Humor of an era in the Area of the 1000 Islands*, (Alexandria Bay; published by the author, 1985), pp. 11–12.

6   Anne Wolcott, in an untitled article about Little Cedar Island, printed in Susan Manes's, *Who's Up?*, (self-published, 1981), p. 149.

7   Brockville historian Doug Grant says there's a dispute about who actually carved the statue. He says that the architect left notes (now in the Metropolitan Toronto Library) that he got the cedar log in a swamp and had a Toronto artist carve the statue. Although Grant says there's no evidence to settle the issue, Holmes, as a local man, is usually credited with carving the statue.

BIBLIOGRAPHY

SUGGESTED READING

The best general introduction to the Thousand Islands is Don Ross's guide *St. Lawrence Islands National Park*. Ross's book is reliable and well researched. It covers a lot of ground in a small space and isn't limited to the national park, as the title suggests. Two of the most intriguing books about the Thousand Islands are *Kingston! Oh Kingston!*, a fat collection of historical accounts edited by Arthur Britton Smith, and *Grindstone: An Island World Remembered*, by Stanley Norcom. Smith's book shows how people from different eras viewed the area, and was useful in preparing this guide book. The work on Grindstone Island is fascinating because it is one of the few books that explores the character of an island community. Another interesting book, though hard to find, is D.D. Calvin's 1945 work, *A Saga of the St. Lawrence: Timber & Shipping Through Three Generations*. Finally, there are the author's two previous books, *River Rats: The People of the Thousand Islands* and *River's Edge: Reprobates, Rum-runners and Other Folk of the Thousand Islands*. Those two books are based on one hundred and fifty interviews with the people of the river and were the basis for some of the conclusions drawn in this guide book.

SOURCES

Angus, Margaret. *The Old Stones of Kingston: Its Buildings Before 1867.* Toronto: University of Toronto Press, 1966.

Barnes, Kathie and Thomas J. Martello. "Businesses Started With 'Wet' Money," *Watertown Daily Times,* August 11, 1983.

Bellomo, J. Jerald. "Upper Canadian Attitudes Towards Crime and Punishment (1832–1851)," *Ontario Historical Society,* Vol. 64, 1972, pp. 11-26.

Bickelhaupt, Valera. "The Denner Brothers All Served in Law Enforcement," *Thousand Islands Sun,* September 9, 1987.

Bogardus, Lorraine B. *River Reflections: A Short History of Morristown.* Worcester, Massachusetts: Danbe Press, 1988.

Bond, Major C.C. J. "The British Base at Carleton Island," *Ontario History,* Vol. LII, No. 1, March 1960, pp. 1-16.

Boyce, Betsy Dewar. *The Rebels of Hastings.* Toronto: University of Toronto Press, 1992.

Boyesen, Persis Yates. "The French and Indian Settlement at Ogdensburg," *The Quarterly: Official Publication of the St. Lawrence County Historical Association,* January 1990, pp. 4-10.

————. "French Personnel at La Presentation," *The Quarterly: Official Publication of the St. Lawrence County Historical Association,* January 1990, pp. 11-15.

Brown, Jack. *Simon Johnston and the Ships of Clayton.* Mallorytown, Ont.: River Heritage Books, 1988.

Buildings of Architectural and Historic Significance. Vol. 1. Kingston: City of Kingston, 1971.

Calvin, D.D. *A Saga of the St. Lawrence: Timber & Shipping Through Three Generations.* Toronto: Ryerson Press, 1945.

Cape Vincent Historical Tour. Cape Vincent: Cape Vincent Improvement League, n.d.

Carr-Harris, Major G.G.M. "The Girouard Story," Vol. I, 1876–1918 of *As You Were! Ex-Cadets Remember.* Ed. Guy C. Smith. Kingston: Royal Military College Club of Canada, 1984.

Casler, Nelie Horton. *Cape Vincent and Its History.* Watertown, N.Y.: Hungerford Holbrook Co., 1906.

"Clinking Bottles Get Canadians Into Trouble," *Thousand Islands Sun,* October 21, 1920.

Clow, H. Meribeth. *Leeds & Grenville Bicentennial 1984.* Brockville: United
Counties of Leeds and Grenville, 1984.

Cole, Larry. "Profile: Archie Garlach — Veteran Cape Fisherman
Tells...[incomplete]," *Watertown Daily Times,* July 31, 1980.

Colombo, John Robert. *Colombo's Canadian References.* Toronto: Oxford
University Press, 1976.

Cook, Garrett. "What Really Happened to the Fort and its Site?" *The
Quarterly: Official Publication of the St. Lawrence County Historical Association,*
January 1990, pp. 15-21.

Cosgrove, Winston M. *Wolfe Island: Past and Present.* Kingston: 1973.

Eves, Sanford Sydney. *Simcoe Island — An Eves Perspective: A Chronicle of the
Island and Its People.* Cobourg: Sanford Eves, 1994.

Fleming, Patsy. "In search of HMCS St. Lawrence: Kingston's Great Man o'
War," *The Kingston Whig-Standard,* March 17, 1995.

————. "Kingston on Foot: Recherche Goods," *The Kingston Whig-Standard
Companion,* January 29, 1994.

Flynn, Louis J. *Built on a Rock: The Story of the Roman Catholic Church in
Kingston 1826–1976.* Kingston: The Roman Catholic Archdiocese of
Kingston, 1976.

Francis, Douglas R., Richard Jones and Donald B. Smith. *Origins: Canadian
History to Confederation.* Toronto: Holt, Rinehart and Winston, 1988.

Godsell, Patricia, ed. *Letters & Diaries of Lady Durham.* : Oberson, 1979.

Gogo, Jean L., ed. *Lights on the St. Lawrence.* Idaho: Caxton Printers Ltd.,
1958.

Green, Ernest. "Corvettes of New France," *The Ontario Historical Society's
Papers and Records,* Vol. XXXV, 1943, pp. 3-12.

Haddock, John A. *A Souvenir of the Thousand Islands of the Saint Lawrence River,
from Kingston to Cape Vincent to Morristown and Brockville.* Alexandria Bay,
N.Y.: Weed-Parsons Printing Co., 1896.

————. *The routes pursued by the excursion steamers upon the Saint Lawrence
River from Clayton and Gananoque to Westminster....* Albany, N.Y.: Weed-
Parsons Printing Co., c. 1895.

Halpenny, Frances G., ed. *Dictionary of Canadian Biography.* Vol. V, 1801–1820,
Toronto: University of Toronto Press, 1983.

Hawke, H. William. *Historic Gananoque.* Belleville: Mika Publishing, 1974.

Hennessy, Peter. " 'So Irksome and So Terrible,' " *The Beaver,* February/March
1991, pp. 12-20.

Hill, Vernon. " 'Dry Days': Man Rehashes Bootlegging years," *Watertown Daily Times*, November 22, 1983.

Hough, Franklin B. *History of St. Lawrence and Franklin Counties, New York.* Albany: Little & Company, 1853; rpt. Baltimore: Regional Publishing Company, 1970.

Hunt, Claude William. *Booze, Boats and Billions: Smuggling Liquid Gold!* Toronto: McClelland and Stewart, 1988.

Innis, Mary Quayle, ed. *Mrs. Simcoe's Diary.* Toronto: Macmillan of Canada and New York: St Martin's Press, 1965.

Jasen, Patricia. "From Nature to Culture: The St. Lawrence River Panorama in Nineteenth-century Ontario Tourism," *Ontario History*, Vol. LXXXV, No.1, March 1993, pp. 43-63.

Jussim, Estelle. *Frederic Remington, the Camera & the Old West.* Fort Worth, Texas: Amon Carter Museum, 1983.

Kaplan, Fred, *Dickens: A Biography.* New York: Avon Books, 1988.

Kilbourn, William. *The Firebrand: William Lyon Mackenzie and the Rebellion in Upper Canada.* Toronto: Clarke, Irwin & Company, 1964.

Leavitt, Thad. W.H. *History of Leeds and Grenville, From 1749 to 1879.* Belleville: Mika Silk Screening Ltd, 1972.

Lewis, Walter Richard. " 'Until Further Notice' The Royal Mail Line and the Passenger Steamboat Trade on Lake Ontario and the Upper St. Lawrence River" 1838–1875. M.A. thesis, Queen's University, Department of History, 1983.

Lucas, Roger S. *Boldt Castle, Heart Island.* Cheektowaga, N.Y.: Research View Publications, n.d.

———. *Research Review.* New York: Roger S. Lucas, 1983.

Lyman, Nicholas J. " 'River Rat' Bootleggers Kept the North Toasting," *Watertown Daily Times*, July 7, 1977.

Malcomson, Bob. "HMS St. Lawrence: Commodore Yeo's Unique First-rate," *Fresh Water*, Vol. 6, No. 2, 1991, pp. 27-36.

Manes, Susan, ed. *Who's Up?*, 1981.

Mangiacasale, Angela. "Wolfe Island: The World Across the Water," *The Kingston Whig-Standard Magazine*, July 10, 1982.

Manley, Atwood and Margaret Manley Mangum. *Frederic Remington and The North Country.* New York: E.P. Dutton, 1988.

"Many Divers Searched For Sir Robert Peel," *Thousand Islands Sun*, 1938.

Markham, Felix. *Napoleon.* Toronto: Mentor Books, 1966.

Martello, Thomas J. "Agent's Lot was Pitiable," *Watertown Daily Times*, August 11, 1983.

McKenzie, Ruth. *Leeds and Grenville: Their First Two Hundred Years*. Toronto: McClelland and Stewart, 1967.

McKnight, Lee. "An Early Bird's View of Prescott Area," unpublished manuscript, The Forwarder's Museum, Prescott, n.d.

———. "Water Street — 'Cradle of Prescott,'" in *Prescott, 1810–1967*, Prescott: The Prescott Journal, 1967.

McLeod, W.J. "Canada's Greatest Prison," *The Canadian Magazine*, Vol. VI, No. 1, November, 1895.

Mika, Nick and Helma. *Kingston City Hall*. Belleville: Mika Publishing, n.d.

Murat, Ines. *Napoleon and the American Dream*. Trans. Frances Frenaye. Baton Rouge: Louisiana State University Press, 1981.

Nalon, John. *A History of Gananoque: The Story of the Town with Photographs*. Gananoque: The Gananoque Museum Board, 1985.

Norcom, Stanley. *Grindstone: An Island World Remembered*. Edited by Norvin Hein. New Cumberland, Penn.: Robert Edwards, 1993.

Nulton, Laurie Ann. *The Golden Age of the Thousand Islands: Its People and Its Castles*. Binghamton: 1981.

Old Fort Henry: the Citadel of Upper Canada. Kingston: The St. Lawrence Parks Commission, 1986.

Osborne, Brian S. and Donald Swainson. *Kingston: Building on the Past*. Westport: Butternut Press, 1988.

Otto, Stephen A., and Richard M. Dumbrille. *Maitland: A Very Neat Village Indeed*. Erin: Boston Mills Press, 1985.

Patterson, William J. *Courage Faith and Love: The History of St. Mark's Church, Barriefield, Ontario*. Barriefield: St. Mark's Church, 1993.

Perkins, Mary Ellen. *A Guide to Provincial Plaques in Ontario*. Toronto: The Ontario Heritage Foundation, 1989.

Pierce, Richard A. "Nils von Schoultz — The Man they had to Hang," *Historic Kingston*, No. 19, February, 1971, pp. 56-65.

Preston, R.A. "The History of the Port of Kingston," *Historic Kingston*, No. 3, November, 1954, pp. 3-25.

"Prison for Kingston Strongly Opposed." *The Kingston Whig-Standard*, October 29, 1958.

"Prohibition Officers Make Raids," *Thousand Islands Sun*, July 14, 1932.

"Prohibition Officers Make Second Raid," *Thousand Islands Sun*, July 21, 1932.

Register of British Shipping: Inland Waters, 1854. Toronto: Geo. E. Thomas & Co.

Richardsons' Chartbook and Cruising Guide. Evanston, Illinois: Richardsons' Marine Publishing, 1993.

Roberts, Taylor. " 'Wicked Moments': Mark Twain in Brockville, Ontario, 1885," *Brockville Museum Monitor,* Vol. 8, No. 1, April 1993.

Ross, Don. *St. Lawrence Islands National Park.* Vancouver and Toronto: Douglas & McIntyre, 1983.

Rush, Laurie W. "In the Wake of the War [of 1812]: Maritime Construction and Commerce in the Nineteenth-century Towns of the Borderlands," in Jan M. Saltzgaber, ed., *A Shared Heritage: The Historical Legacy of Sackets Harbor and Madison Barracks.* Ithaca, N.Y.: Ithaca College, 1993, pp. 55-62.

Samuels, Peggy and Harold. *Frederic Remington: A Biography.* Garden City, N.Y.: Doubleday and Company, 1982.

Shapiro, Michael Edward, and Peter H. Hassrick, eds. *Frederic Remington: The Masterworks.* New York: Abradale Press, 1991.

Shipping news from the [Kingston] Chronicle and Gazette and Weekly Commercial Advertiser in the mid-1800s. Typed manuscript, Marine Museum of the Great Lakes, Kingston.

Smith, Arthur Britton, ed. *Kingston! Oh Kingston!* Kingston: Brown & Martin, 1987.

Smith, Donald B. *Sacred Feathers: The Reverend Peter Jones (Kahkewaquonaby) and the Mississauga Indians.* Toronto: University of Toronto Press, 1987.

———. "Who Are The Mississauga?" *Ontario History,* Vol. LXVII, No. 4, December, 1975, pp. 211-222.

Smith, Douglas N.W. *By Rail, Road and Water to Gananoque.* Ottawa: Douglas N.W. Smith, 1995.

Smith, Marjorie. "Timothy Buckly 1783–1867," *Pioneer People and Places,* Early Grenville, Vol. 5, n.d.

Smith, Susan Weston. *The First Summer People: The Thousand Islands 1650–1910.* Erin: Boston Mills Press, 1993.

Snider, C.H.J. *Tarry Breeks and Velvet Garters.* Toronto: Ryerson Press, 1958.

Spankie, R.M. "Wolfe Island, Past and Present," *Proceedings of the New York State Historical Association.* Vol. XIII, c. 1914, pp. 210-249.

Stanley, George F.G. *Conflicts and Social Notes: The War of 1812–1814, The Patriot War — 1837/38.* Mallorytown Landing: Parks Canada, 1976.

———. "The Battle of the Windmill," *Historic Kingston,* No. 3, November, 1954, pp. 41-56.

————. "William Johnston: Pirate or Patriot?" *Historic Kingston*, No. 6, December, 1957, pp. 13-28.

———— and Richard A. Preston. *A Short History of Kingston as a Military and Naval Centre*. Kingston:[Royal Military College], n.d.

Stewart, J. Douglas, Ian E. Wilson, et al. *Heritage Kingston*. Kingston: Agnes Etherington Art Centre, 1973.

Stacton, David. *The Bonapartes*. New York: Simon and Schuster, 1966.

Swainson, Donald. *Garden Island: A Shipping Empire*. Kingston: Marine Museum of the Great Lakes, [n.d.].

Thompson, Shawn. "Dickens letter found and lost," *The Kingston Whig-Standard*, November 26, 1994.

————. "19th-century latrine reveals secrets of fort life." *The Kingston Whig-Standard*, July 12, 1991.

————. "River pilots put to the test," *The Kingston Whig-Standard*, September 3, 1993.

————. *River Rats: The People of The Thousand Islands*. Burnstown: General Store Publishing House, 1989.

————. *River's Edge: Reprobates, Rum-runners and Other Folk of The Thousand Islands*. Burnstown: General Store Publishing House, 1991.

Thwaites, Reuben Gold, ed. *The Jesuit Relations and Allied Documents: Travels and Explorations of the Jesuit Missionaries in New France, 1610–1791*. Cleveland: The Burrows Brothers, 1901.

"View of Kingston Penitentiary," *The Dominion Illustrated*, Vol. VI, No. 142, March 21, 1891.

Webster's American Biographies. Springfield, Mass.: G & C Merriam Co., 1974.

White, Arthur V. *Long Sault Rapids, St. Lawrence River: An Enquiry into the Constitutional and Other Aspects of the Project to Develop Power Therefrom*. Committee on Waters and Water-powers, Commission of Conservation Canada. Ottawa: Mortimer Co., 1913.

Wilder, Patrick. *Seaway Trail Guidebook to the War of 1812*. Oswego: Seaway Trail Inc., 1987.

Wilson, Ian E. et al. *Kingston City Hall*. Kingston: Corporation of the City of Kingston, 1974.

Young, Anna G. *Great Lakes' Saga: The Influence of One Family on the Development of Canadian Shipping on the Great Lakes 1816–1931*. Owen Sound: Richardson, Bond and Wright Ltd., 1965.

ACKNOWLEDGMENTS

The author wishes to give special thanks to the following people, who not only helped with information, but read parts of the manuscript and made suggestions to improve it: Maurice Smith, director of the Marine Museum of the Great Lakes in Kingston; Donald Smith, historian and specialist in the history of First Nations People, the University of Calgary; Ken Robinson, acting chief of visitor activities, St. Lawrence Islands National Park; J. Ross McKenzie, museum curator, Royal Military College of Canada; David St. Onge, curator of the Kingston Penitentiary Museum; John M. Davison, chief of visitor activities, Fort Wellington National Historic Site, Prescott; Phoebe Tritton, research librarian at the Clayton Antique Boat Museum; Doug Grant, history teacher, Brockville; Richard M. Dumbrille, historian, Maitland; Persis Boyesen, official historian for the city of Ogdensburg.

The author also wishes to thank the following people for the generous help they gave: Dave Warner, superintendent of the Thousand Islands National Park; Keith Dewar, former chief of visitor activities at the St. Lawrence Islands National Park and now a lecturer in New Zealand; Laura Foster, curator, the Frederic Remington Art Museum, Ogdensburg; Deborah Emerton, director, Brockville Museum; Russell Wilcox, executive director of the Thousand Islands Bridge Authority; Bill Danforth, director of the Clayton Antique Boat Museum; Roger Lucas, biographer of George Boldt; Cheryl McMullen, curator of The Forwarders' Museum, Prescott; John Nalon, president of the Gananoque Historical Society; Lynette McLennan, curator, Gananoque Museum; Hazel McMane, town of Alexandria historian; Lorraine B. Bogardus, town historian, Morristown; Charles Dunham, former Jefferson County historian; Steve McCready, historian, Fort Henry; Nina Comins, Cape Vincent town historian; John N. Russell, general manager, Bonnie Castle Resort; Jeff Hebert, owner of the Edgewood Resort; Captain Harold Hogan, Kingston; Doug Duncan, Kingston; Bill Harpell, Barriefield; Bill Tooker, Brockville; Ramona and Lyle Nunn, Wellesley Island; Ethel Johnston, Rockport; Gerald Roney, Hill Island; R.F. Fawcett, Wolfe Island; Buck Mullin, Wolfe Island; Rachael Horne, Wolfe Island; John D'Esterre, Garden Island; Edwin A. Livingston, geneologist; Louise Strong, Morristown; George Eves, Simcoe Island; Maureen Brady, Liverpool, New York; Monica O'Connor Brady, Penn Yan, New York; Peter Van Lent, Canton, New York; Tom O'Connor, Almonte; Alex Marshall, Howe Island; Tom Marshall, Howe Island; Captain Larry Hickey, Cape Vincent.

And, of course, thanks to the author's wife, Brenda, for her love and support through the tribulations of working on a book.

INDEX